Advanced Praise for *Killer Brands*

"Our company has increased its market value from $100 million to $1 billion using the ideas in this bool[...] if I get one usable idea from it. With [...] at least fifteen concepts from the book [...] innovative marketers I have ever know[...]
—Zan Guerry, CEO, [...]

"This book is better than an MBA in marketing. Frank Lane's book will help you create your own Killer Brand and build your business. One of the smartest marketers I know. (And I know a lot)."
—Peter Larson, retired chairman and CEO, Brunswick, and formerchairman of the Consumer Segment of Johnson & Johnson, Princeton, NJ

"I created and executed the original branding strategy for Microsoft which included the naming and positioning of Windows. I credit my success at Microsoft to Frank. Prior to Microsoft I worked for Frank as vice president of marketing for Neutrogena. At Neutrogena, Frank exposed me to many of the concepts that he has now documented in *Killer Brands*. I successfully applied these concepts at Microsoft."
—Rowland Hanson, cofounder and CEO, The HansonMaslen Group, Seattle, WA

"Frank Lane has the best marketing mind I've ever encountered. His understanding of the value of a strong brand and the requirements to build a Killer Brand are second to none. Frank has the unique talent to articulate those strengths and requirements in such a way that anyone can understand and appreciate."
—Rod Sands, president and COO, Silver Ventures, and co-creator of Pace Picante Sauce, San Antonio, TX

"*Killer Brands* is one of those unusual business books: it is educational *and* entertaining. Relevant to both experts and laypersons, *Killer Brands* is an insightful primer on the concept of brands and the importance of creating a compelling and differentiated expectation. If you want to become the product or service of first choice for your customers, this book is essential reading."
—Sergio J. Masvidal, vice chairman, American Express Bank, and head of Global Wealth Management, Miami, FL

"Frank Lane shared his Killer Brand principles and helped us apply them to our work in philanthropy, bringing the kind of discovery, vision, courage, know-how, and tenacity that characterize the social entrepreneurial projects that we seek to fund. He helped us apply to ourselves the kind of analytical thinking and strategic discipline that we now demand of grantees."

—Alberto Ibarguen, CEO, Knight Foundation, Miami, FL

"Killer reading for anyone interested in building his or her brand while also building his or her career . . . written by one of the masters of big-time, classical branding."

—George Winston, retired senior vice president of
Grey Advertising, Los Angeles, CA

"Every once in a great while, you run into someone who is brilliant at his or her profession. Frank Lane is brilliant at marketing. Every leader who is pressured for margin and revenue growth needs to buy this book for themselves and for each person in their marketing department."

—Patrick Riha, vice president,
Roundhouse Marketing and Promotions, Madison, WI

"Artists are told we are not 'salesmen' and that to work on becoming one would be to lose our integrity. Thus, we deny that our aim is to sell our photographs, our paintings, our talents, or our personalities to others. This book has helped me crystallize my difference. And that in turn frees me to amplify that difference and to do even greater art."

—Sherry Mills, multimedia artist, New York, NY

"Others can discuss marketing and branding principles but Frank Lane can uniquely relate to them through real-life experience. His common-sense principles for building a Killer Brand clearly demonstrate the path for unparalleled success."

—Barry Goldblatt, director, marketing research,
Church & Dwight Co., Inc, Princeton, NJ

"I really enjoyed reading *Killer Brands*. It is very easy to follow, well organized, and the examples about specific brands are extremely helpful. I especially like that one without any branding experience (such as myself) can read it and still understand it."

—Kate Goodwin, marketing intern,
senior at Centennial High School, Atlanta, GA

KILLER BRANDS

KILLER BRANDS

Create and Market a Brand That Will Annihilate the Competition

FRANK LANE

BUSINESS

Avon, Massachusetts

This book is dedicated to two of my work associates, Joshua Lane and Rhonda McHardy, who motivated me to "Write it all down."

Published by
Adams Media, an F+W Publications Company
57 Littlefield Street, Avon, MA 02322. U.S.A.
www.adamsmedia.com

ISBN 10: 1-59869-123-6
ISBN 13: 978-1-59869-123-8

Printed in Canada.

J I H G F E D C B A

Library of Congress Cataloging-in-Publication Data
is available from the publisher.

This publication is designed to provide accurate and authoritative information with regard to the subject matter covered. It is sold with the understanding that the publisher is not engaged in rendering legal, accounting, or other professional advice. If legal advice or other expert assistance is required, the services of a competent professional person should be sought.
—From a *Declaration of Principles* jointly adopted by a Committee of the American Bar Association and a Committee of Publishers and Associations

Many of the designations used by manufacturers and sellers to distinguish their product are claimed as trademarks. Where those designations appear in this book and Adams Media was aware of a trademark claim, the designations have been printed with initial capital letters.

This book is available at quantity discounts for bulk purchases. For information, please call 1-800-289-0963.

CONTENTS

Acknowledgments

I would like to thank William "Budge" Wallis, Gary Krebs, Shoshanna Grossman, Larry Shea, Paula Munier, my copyeditor Suzanne Goraj, and everyone at Adams Media; all of my clients and coworkers who over the years actually taught me all that is in this book; and Jessica Lane for serving as my research associate and first editor.

INTRODUCTION

Owning a Killer Brand can change your life. You can find hundreds of books on branding, and legions of companies and consultancies that practice branding. But what you will learn in this book is that there is a world of difference between the advantages inherent in ordinary branding and the raw power of what we might call "branding to the nth degree," or creating a true Killer Brand.

What Is a True "Killer Brand"?

A *Killer Brand* exists when an entity derives a disproportionate amount of success in its category because of a compelling and differentiated expectation that comes to be associated with its name. A true Killer Brand will be chosen over competing brands—in any category, in any country, at any time, and often at any reasonable price.

While this book is about the battle of brands in the marketplace, the ideas you'll find here on how consumers make choices, along with the three Killer Brand principles, can be adapted to any situation where it is in your best interest to manage the choices of other people. Pay close attention to that idea: "where it is in your best interest to manage the choices of other people." These principles will not only work in your business, but also with your career in general, your social life, your family, your children, and more.

This book is organized into five parts:

✳ Part One first gives you the reasons *why* you should want a Killer Brand. It goes on to explain how the world works on just *two* principles. The first is the principle of **Choice.** The second is the principle of **Expectation.**
✳ Parts Two through Four demonstrate how Killer Brands work. You'll discover the *three* principles that will show you how to

xi

create a Killer Brand of your own in any business, in any market, anywhere in the world. These principles are **Focus, Alignment,** and **Linkage.**

✳ Finally, in Part Five, we'll put it all together to show Killer Brands in action. We'll explore some examples of how to create and expand a Killer Brand, along with some cautionary tales of brands that have at least temporarily lost their way.

What can a Killer Brand do for you? Let me put it this way. When you seriously set out to create and own a Killer Brand, and you then execute the three elegant steps in this book with precision, consistency, and brilliance, this is what will happen: You will unlock the marketplace and create brands that annihilate the competition. I am not kidding. You will *annihilate* the competition.

Your brand will become a Killer Brand. And a Killer Brand will beat other brands time and time and time again.

You will become a marketing legend. Your resume will feature so many big success stories that even your mother will be proud of you. You will be hounded at cocktail circles and dinner parties. Everyone will want to talk to you. You will become a brand celebrity. You may even get rich. You will become a marketing star . . . a very bright marketing star.

PART ONE

WHY YOU SHOULD WANT A KILLER BRAND

1

The Power of a Killer Brand

Would you rather own a me-too product with no way to compete except on price, or would you rather own a Killer Brand, something that is recognized as different in a way that compels people to choose it and use it, makes people ask for it and wait for it, even if the price is a little higher? The choice is up to you.

If you want to own a me-too product, you can put this book down now and just start lowering your price. If you would rather own a Killer Brand, keep reading.

The U.S. market is filled with hundreds of thousands of branded products and branded services, and that is not even counting all of the local independent ideas and small chains in every market in the country. America has greater choice in every category than any culture in the history of the world. I have even been told that there are more mutual funds (which are a form of financial brands) in the United States than there are individual stocks trading on all of the country's stock exchanges. How's that for a crowded market?

Businesspeople from other countries that I've worked with are all stunned by the level of competition in America. But America is no longer alone. Other developed countries around the world are becoming gorged with the same surfeit of competition. Out of these hundreds of thousands of competing brands, how many of them conform to the Killer Brand definition? How many of them are built on the three Killer Brand principles in this book? How many of them qualify as true Killer Brands?

The answer is very few, far less than 1 percent. That is why owning a Killer Brand amounts to having an almost unfair advantage over the competition.

Once again, answer the question for yourself. Would you rather own a product or service that is nothing more than me-too, with no way to compete except on price or on broader availability or greater amount of marketing dollars spent, or would you rather own a Killer Brand, recognized as different in a way that compels people to choose it and use it, makes people ask for it and wait for it, even at a higher price?

Owning a Killer Brand Will Change Your Business and Your Life

All you have to do is know how the world works and learn how to use the three key principles in this book and you can dominate any category. You can beat any competitor.

It makes no difference whether you are selling ice cream, a dress shop, secretarial services, coffee, software, private banking, hotels, laundry detergent, lottery tickets, or racehorses. The principles that you are going to learn are category-neutral. They work on everything.

Your success will have nothing to do with the size of your organization, or the size of your company. It will have nothing to do with the size of your budget, the size of the opportunity, or the strength of the competition.

Your success will depend on the size of your intellect and the strength of your discipline. Your understanding of how the world works *(Choice* and *Expectation)* and your use of the three Killer Brand principles *(Focus—Alignment—Linkage)* in sequential steps will act like a cryptogram for the marketplace. Use them adeptly and unlock the real magic of marketing.

Creating a Killer Brand Is Simple but Difficult

> *A Killer Brand exists when an entity derives a disproportionate amount of success in its category because of a compelling and differentiated expectation that comes to be associated with its name.*

Let's start with the premise brought up in the Introduction, as stated in the box at right.

Sounds simple doesn't it? It is simple, but it is also very difficult.

What do I mean by that? Think of it this way: Tasks can be either simple or complicated, and they can be either easy or difficult. There are four combinations: simple and easy, simple but difficult, complicated but easy, and complicated and difficult.

The task of creating a Killer Brand falls into the category of simple but difficult. What makes it simple? There are only *two* things to understand about how the world works (**Choice** and **Expectation**), and *three* steps for creating a Killer Brand (**Focus, Alignment,** and **Linkage**). Just five concepts altogether, but they are extremely powerful when skillfully used. What makes it difficult is that each concept is subtle and rich with possibilities. There are many options and choices within each concept. You are going to learn each concept inside and out—its importance, its meaning, its subtleties—and then use your knowledge to create a Killer Brand.

Here's a quick summary:

✳ Every dollar that you will ever make depends on Choice—in fact, every dollar depends upon a chain of choices on the behalf of your product or service.

✳ Every Choice that will be made will be based on Expectation. This is the way the world works. Deliver the right expectation and get chosen.

✳ Focus is that one singular, differentiating, and powerfully compelling quality, that motivating Expectation that your Killer Brand is going to become known for . . . not just because of what it says it does, but because it also does what it says.

✳ Alignment is connecting everything that you do in perfect harmony to deliver that Focus consistently time after time, user after user, making sure that nothing you do inadvertently detracts from that Focus or detracts from that expectation.

✳ **Linkage** is finding a way to get that Focus, that expectation credited in the minds of your prospects to the name of your Killer Brand and to no other brand.

You can create the perfectly differentiated and compelling focus, align everything perfectly, but get no brand credit for it, and fall woefully short. If you miss this last step, Linkage, you will never have a Killer Brand. But when you *focus* on the right expectation, engineer perfect *alignment*, and create memorable *linkage* to the name of your brand, then get ready for the fireworks. When it all comes together it is like marketplace mojo—magic.

Dominant Versus Killer Brands

Using the principles in this book, you can start from a zero budget and create a Killer Brand. I know because I have created a Killer Brand as an entrepreneur. I have also created a Killer Brand in a small company. And I have created a Killer Brand in a large company.

You too can have a Killer Brand. It may or may not dominate its category because niche brands can be Killer Brands also.

What's the difference between a *Killer Brand* and a *dominant brand?* The main one is this: A dominant brand requires the expenditure of significant resources over time—marketing investment, infrastructure, people, etc. By contrast, as I've just mentioned, a Killer Brand can be created by organizations large and small, and with little initial investment.

Coca-Cola is a good example of a dominant brand, but it does not fit the definition of a Killer Brand because it has never been differentiated enough to meet all of the principles of the concept. In fact, there are parts of the world where Coca-Cola is not number one, and these are not just places where **Pepsi** surpasses Coke. In the Caribbean, there is a cola brand out of Trinidad that behaves more like a Killer Brand than does Coca Cola. It's called **Chubby Cola,** and on many islands it is the market leader.

BRAND NAMES THAT STAND OUT

Throughout this book, the first time a brand name is mentioned it will be in **bold type.** And at the back of the book, besides a regular subject index you'll find a brand index listing all the brands we'll discuss here.

Nike is another dominant brand, but overall it does not fit the definition of a Killer Brand because it is too diffuse to have a genuinely compelling and differentiated expectation. Certainly Nike has had items within its line that operated consistently with the principles in this book. For instance, **Air Jordans** fit our definition of a Killer Brand. But the majority of the brand's strength comes from dominant investment.

I am not suggesting that owning a dominant brand is not a valuable situation. I am just saying that a brand does not have to be dominant to be very valuable. Some dominant brands got there by being a Killer Brand first, but many did it with force of effort and dominant resources such as infrastructures, sales forces, trade clout, heavy marketing investment in sampling and advertising, and other very expensive tools.

In this book, we will concentrate on what makes a Killer Brand while assuming that you are not blessed with dominant resources, financial or otherwise. If you do have access to dominant resources, following the Killer Brand principles will make every dollar you spend at least five or six times more effective. If you don't have dominant resources, following these principles will be the difference between success and failure.

Before you read this book, I do need to warn you. The three Killer Brand principles are so simple that the book may seem elementary. But as simple as these three principles are, in the real world of day-to-day work they prove difficult in practice for us all.

I have been creating brands with the intention of making them Killer Brands for my entire career. This is all I do. And though I place far below Einstein on any measure of intelligence, I didn't just fall off of a turnip truck. Creating brands is just plain hard. It's difficult to find the right focus. It's easy to get sidetracked from it even when you do find it.

I know how to play perfect golf. But I can't *do* it. However, once in a blue moon I have been to that place where every little thing in my swing was perfect, and lo and behold, the ball actually went exactly where I intended. I just can't do it every time.

In golf, if you can execute perfectly more often than your competitors, you can become a Killer Golfer. The same is true in the world of brands.

If you can learn to execute perfectly more often than your competitors, you can become the owner or manager of a Killer Brand.

How to Out-Execute Your Competitors and Create Killer Brands

It all starts with understanding how the world works, and then really understanding the three steps to a Killer Brand. Each step is really a principle that will be explained in all of its simplicity and its complexity. They are referred to as steps because they are best developed sequentially. Throughout this book, you'll also find numerous examples and case histories ("Brand Studies") to help illustrate the important principles you need to understand and implement.

I will sometimes refer to the three Killer Brand principles in this book as the *three keys*. This is because when you use them in sequence—*Focus* first, *Alignment* second, and *Linkage* third—the principles work just like the three-number combination lock you once used on your high-school locker. They work like *The Da Vinci Code* (a recently introduced book that has become a Killer Brand). All of a sudden the marketplace just opens for you. You and your business are off to the races. You will own a Killer Brand, and everyone else will be reeling before your daunting market presence.

What you are going to learn in this book is not new. While I was in college in the mid-sixties, I watched these three keys produce a Killer Brand for a tiny little South Carolina company called Texize. This company was like David up against the Goliaths of Procter & Gamble, Lever, and Colgate.

BRAND STUDY: Putting a Janitor in a Drum

Texize's Killer Brand was **Janitor in a Drum**. The brand took the market by storm, like an overnight tornado. Its *focus* was the first "industrial strength" cleaner for the home. Its *alignment* was so perfect that even the packaging was a miniature, green industrial drum replicated in plastic, and of course the *linkage* in this case was also right in the name, Janitor in a Drum. I can still hear the clanking noises in the TV ad made by the forklift choosing and lifting a drum of cleaner in the factory as the drum morphed visually into a retail package of Janitor in a Drum, one that looked just like the industrial drum.

Janitor in a Drum became a leading brand even though, at that time, it was a product from a very small company.

My fellow marketers and I all watched Janitor in a Drum and admired its success, but we did not know about the three keys at that time. They had yet to be codified. But as you should be able to see from just the brief description above, Janitor in a Drum was a perfect example of executing the three keys that we now recognize—*Focus*, *Alignment*, and *Linkage*. It's the first example of a Killer Brand that I remember from my own marketing life, even though I had nothing to do with it.

Did owning Janitor in a Drum change the life of Texize? You bet it did.

Before Janitor, Texize was a small industrial cleaning company in Greenville, South Carolina. Janitor catapulted the company into the limelight. Their next big innovation was **Spray 'n Wash,** which started what is now an almost $1 billion category. Texize was later acquired by Dow Chemicals. Its shareholders made a lot of money. And Tommy Greer, the son of the founder and the Texize President at the time of the development and introduction of these great brands, went on to invent the **Universal Product Code** (UPC), the bar code that allowed retailers around the world to computerize their checkout and inventory control.

BRAND STUDY: The Spanx Story

For those of you who prefer learning from the present rather than from the past, here's the story I offer of what I believe is a recently emerging potential Killer Brand.

When I first heard of **Spanx** and saw it in a store, my immediate thought was this: Why the devil didn't I think of that? It's probably because I am not a woman, and almost certainly also because I am not as clever as Sara Blakely. This is a truly remarkable story.

What's a woman to do with a beautiful pair of cream-colored, form-fitting pants that show every possible bodily imperfection and panty line, particularly when she wants to wear open-toed shoes?

If you are the entrepreneur and inventor Sara Blakely, and you find no footless, body-shaping pantyhose to be had anywhere in 1998, you cut the feet off a good pair of control top pantyhose and make your own. Voila! No more unsightly visible panty lines and bulges, or the big no-no of pantyhose showing in your peek-a-boo shoes. You stand with confidence.

And stand up with confidence is just what Sara Blakely did—both for a living and for a product she really believed in. First she conceived and made the prototype for Spanx, and then she peddled it by modeling its unique benefits personally, with before-and-after demos that included sporting those cream-colored pants and lifting her pant legs repeatedly to show potential retail buyers what Spanx could do for their customers. And then she would spend all day lifting her pant legs and showing customers what it could do for them. She and her friends constantly called media outlets to trumpet her innovation, which resulted in significant media coverage. Though this tactic was originally done in part because of a lack of money for advertising, it was an approach that worked like gangbusters. Spanx's best form of advertising—then and now—was word of mouth.

But first things first. Ms. Blakely says on her Web site, *www. spanx.com,* "Working as a sales trainer by day and performing stand-up comedy at night, I didn't know the first thing about the pantyhose industry (except I dreaded wearing most pantyhose). Also, I had never taken a business class which made the process even more challenging. As a result, I had only one source to operate from . . . my gut." But in her gut, she believed she had a product that women wanted and needed.

After developing an innovative product, she set about giving it a memorable name. She thought about the fact that **Kodak** and Coca-Cola are two of the most recognizable brand names in the world and that both have a predominant "K" sound. From her work as a standup comic, she knew that the "K" sound makes people laugh. Using this knowledge, she wanted to have a "K" in her brand's name for luck. She changed her original choice of the name SPANKS to spelling it with an "X" after last-minute research pointed out that made-up words are not only easier to trademark but work better as product names than real words do. Sara says that "Spanx is edgy, fun, extremely catchy, and for a moment it makes your mind wander (admit it). Plus it's all about making women's butts look better, so why not?" I'd have to agree.

Off to a really good start, Sara still had a lot of homework to do. And so she did her homework—first doing a great deal of Internet research on trademarks and patents (specifically, pantyhose patents) and then running her business from her own apartment, using $5,000 of her own savings. She wrote her own patent application and got it approved, successfully trademarked the name Spanx online, and then made her first prototype of Spanx Original Footless Pantyhose and stood up for it, time and time again, until it had legs of its own.

Finding a manufacturer was the biggest challenge of all, Sara relates on her Web site:

Taking a week off of work, I drove around North Carolina begging mill owners to help make my idea. They always asked the same three questions: "And you are?" "And you are representing?" "And you are financially backed by?" When I answered Sara Blakely to all three, most of them sent me away, not to mention they thought the idea "made no sense, and would never sell." Two weeks later I received a call from a mill owner who said he "decided to help make my crazy idea." When asked why he had the change of heart, he said, "I have two daughters." Turns out they didn't think the idea was crazy at all. The prototype took a year to perfect because as someone who wanted to wear the product every day I was obsessed with comfort.

And sell they did. Once Sara found a manufacturer in 2000, she sold over 50,000 pairs from the back of her apartment in three months' time. Sara Blakely's Spanx revitalized an industry in a ten-year slump, an industry that, prior to her debut, had been a $2 billion male-dominated hosiery industry. She happily exceeded her first year's sales goal of selling 200,000 pairs.

Since their debut, Spanx have been featured in the coveted "Oprah's Favorite Things," after Oprah Winfrey discovered them and admitted that she too had been cutting the feet out of her pantyhose. They have been snapped up by high-end retailers such as **Saks Fifth Avenue, Neiman Marcus, Nordstrom, Bergdorf Goodman, Lord & Taylor,** and **Bloomingdale's,** just to name a few; and they have been featured on *The Oprah Winfrey Show* and CNN, as well as in the pages of *Glamour, Vogue, People, In Style,* the *New York Times, Vanity Fair, Women's Wear Daily,* and *USA Today*. Its selling point is that the Spanx line is designed by a woman for women and "crafted to promote comfort and confidence in women."

Spanx has become a household word for women in the fashion know. By 2005 the company, remaining self-funded, had become a global brand; it continues to show increasing profits, celebrating $85 million in retail sales.

Sara Blakely was named Entrepreneur of the Year for the Southeast Region by Ernst and Young in 2002 and Georgia's Woman of the Year in 2005. She became the runner-up on Sir Richard Branson's reality series *The Rebel Billionaire: Branson's Quest for the Best,* earning her a check for $750,000 from Branson, which has enabled her to pursue her dream of starting a foundation to support and empower women—The Sara Blakely Foundation. A portion of proceeds from her new line

ASSETS, a new slimming line exclusive to Target stores, will benefit Ms. Blakely's foundation.

So what did a lady with a lot of smarts, but no business education and no formal financial backing or brand training, do right to create and own a Killer Brand? Just about everything: identifying her target audience and staying true to them; holding on to her vision of comfortable, slimming garments that minimize figure flaws; using innovative designs and smart features that would continually wow, delight, work for, and win over the women they were made for, thus acquiring loyal customers for life.

What else did Sara do right? Well, how about taking a year to develop a prototype that met her exacting standards and was just right; picking a memorable, differentiated brand name that links to her product's core expectation and to its slogan, "Don't worry, we've got your butt covered"; and using packaging and marketing that is as fresh, fun, and innovative as her line of products and that appeals to its target audience. And then going out and promoting it great guns until she found others who believed in it as much as she did.

Sara has continued to command the attention of fashion editors, television producers, and celebrity stylists by developing and launching more than sixty styles of innovative shapewear through her company, Spanx Inc.—products with names like **Bra-llelujah, Two Timin' Tights, Power Panties, Slim-Cognito,** and **Topless Socks,** all designed to be comfortable, slimming, and stylish.

The Spanx operating philosophy "centers upon delivering the highest levels of quality, comfort, and innovation to women—all with a sense of humor."

The core expectation was "Your butt will look better in skirts and pants." How compelling is that to most women?

Simple Rules

This book will contain lots of examples of brands—like Janitor in a Drum and Spanx—that get it right, as well as examples of brands that get it wrong or just miss by a bit. I'll include perfect examples, disastrous examples, and lots of in-betweens—that dreaded state in which most of the marketplace struggles at any given time.

> Use three simple steps to create Killer Brands that will annihilate the competition.

While writing this book, I was reminded of a story about the great artist Picasso. He was sitting in a restaurant one night and a woman came over and gushed to him, and asked that he draw something for her on her napkin. He obliged, and then asked her for $10,000. She was taken aback and replied, "$10,000? That drawing only took you five minutes!"

Picasso's reply was indignant. "Wrong, Madam! That particular drawing took me forty years!"

The same is, in a way, true here. I have been working in marketing for forty years, and I only discovered the simplicity of the three steps to Killer Brands a few years ago. A client asked me to create a speech for him to deliver in Europe about why brands were important and why they worked. In trying to figure it out and explain it simply, I stumbled upon these three steps.

I have been smarter since I wrote that speech and discovered the three steps than I was in all the previous years combined. If these three steps can teach an old dog like me new tricks, think what they can do for you.

In fact, I have improved my skill set during the writing of this book more than in any similar time frame in my career. First, just trying to write down the concepts and explain them in words that I hope you will understand increased the precision of my thinking. Also, as I wrote this book, I began to realize how much more powerful it can be to think about "expectation" as a replacement for terms that have been used over the years such as "core essence," "USP," "promise," and so on.

I am embarrassed that it took me so many years to discover the simple rules that were right under my nose. But it did. And what a difference that discovery has made for me and my subsequent marketing efforts.

Read this book. Pay attention to it. Practice it. Review it. Use it to measure your efforts. And you will be smarter, too. You will understand how the world works. You will control the three keys to unlocking the marketplace. You will control the keys to the kingdom. You will be able to create and market Killer Brands that annihilate the competition.

2

Control the Chain of Choice

In a free economy, or any economy that is relatively free, the market for anything is basically a cumulative record of individual choices. It all comes down to how many buyers make which choices, and how often they make them.

In fact, I heard a financial speaker once at an Alex Brown FL financial conference claim that there was no such thing as the financial performance of a company, that there was only a financial record of the marketing performance of a company. If a company does not market well, it cannot perform well. It's even been said that marketing is too important to be left to the marketing department. Marketing involves understanding, creating, and managing all of the factors that go into controlling choice . . . and that's because business results are always the function of cumulative choices.

It helps to think of this dynamic as the *Chain of Choice.*

At any given moment, any buyer, whether a consumer or a business, is free to make any choice he, she, or it wishes. Buyers are free to choose your offering or someone else's. They are free to make a good choice. They are free to make a bad choice. They are free to spend as little or as much as they like. In a market like the United States, where credit availability is so broad, buyers are even free to make choices they cannot afford.

So here's the first rule of thumb for becoming a legendary marketer capable of creating and building Killer Brands: Remember that your ultimate goal is to affect choice on behalf of your brand. And that responsibility calls for controlling not just the choices of the end buyer but also hundreds of choices along a path from your desk to the end buyer—and often one choice beyond, by the end user who is sometimes one step beyond the buyer.

> As a marketer, your goal is ultimately to affect choice on behalf of your brand.

For instance, your management is free to choose the size of the budgets to give its various products; your sales force is free to choose which brand to focus on, as well as when and how hard to push it; a distributor is free to choose which products it will carry, at what price it will sell them, how much time it will devote to which products, and how much effort it will put into the selling. A retailer is free to choose which products it will carry, at what prices, where they will be stocked, how much of them will be inventoried, how they will be merchandised or displayed, etc. A retail salesperson is free to choose what she will recommend, what she will say about it, and to whom she will recommend it.

Of course, an end buyer is free to determine what product or service he will choose. Just as important, end buyers are free to choose how often they will buy a product and how much of it they will use after purchase, as well as whether they will recommend the product to someone else or recommend against it. It all hinges on what they think about the product, how they feel about their choice, whether they will make the same choice again, and so on.

Your ultimate business results will depend on cumulative chains of hundreds of choices made over and over again by many different individuals along a spectrum that reaches from your desk to the ultimate behaviors of your end user. That is what I mean when I say that the market is controlled by the Chain of Choice. For example, the fourteenth link in the chain will often not even have an opportunity to make the choice you want him to, if the eighth and tenth members in the chain do not make the right choice further up the chain from him.

Bribery Is Not Marketing

I love the title of Rick Page's book, *Hope Is Not a Strategy: The 6 Keys to Winning the Complex Sale* (McGraw-Hill, 2001), and I love that concept, so I am going to interject a similar thought here: *Bribery Is Not Real Marketing*. I want you to understand how important this principle is.

If you examine the marketing plans and activities of most companies, brands, and executives you meet, you will find an over-reliance on forms of bribery to affect choice along the entire Chain of Choice.

For instance, you will find money spent to motivate sales forces to sell more at a certain time. I am not talking about their salaries and expenses. I am talking about incentives, spifs, contests, etc., used to motivate them to do the job that is outlined on their job description. You will find incremental money (that is, money beyond their commissions) spent to motivate distributors to stock an item and agree to try to sell it.

You will find over half of the money in most marketing budgets allocated to paying the trade channel to carry an item (a practice now euphemistically called "slotting allowances"), or to display or promote an item, etc.

You will find over half of almost anything sold through any form of trade channel sold at some kind of reduced price. In fact, in my twenty-five years of consulting I have found virtually no businesses that do not sell at least half of their revenue at some kind of reduced price or on some kind of price-oriented promotion.

For instance, when I began working for Neutrogena, the company had an accounting system that did not allow for the tracking of the amount of money given to the trade in the form of discounts, etc., because they entered each sale at the net price realized. Sophisticated marketing companies enter every sale at full price and then charge the marketing budget with the difference between full price and the actual sales as a reduced revenue charge.

When I installed this kind of metric measurement at Neutrogena, I found that the company was shipping 73 percent of all of its volume at a reduced price. By tracking this behavior and making certain changes over time, we were able to reduce this 73 percent to 37 percent over three years. All of that money that we were no longer giving away was converted to forms of real marketing: sampling, advertising, consumer promotions, and so on. That incremental investment in real marketing helped us change the annual growth rate of the company from 1.5 percent to 22 percent.

You can find the same phenomenon in business-to-business marketing, perhaps even to a greater degree because many of the sales and contracts are at negotiated prices. In fact, it is sometimes difficult to derive the full price in order to install a metrics system as described for Neutrogena.

But make no mistake, *discounting to control choice is not real marketing*. It is just a form of bribery. And there is a lot of gold deposited by marketers in them thar hills.

A $1 billion carpeting company that I worked with had a net sales accounting system. The marketing budget for the company was $18 million. The sales force had the latitude to execute a transaction at any one of eleven different price levels.

When we finally agreed upon what determined full price, and executed an analysis to determine how much money was represented by the various forms of discounting, we discovered that over $300 million was being given away to control choice, virtually all to the trade channel, virtually none of it to the ultimate carpet purchaser.

That meant the actual marketing budget was not $18 million but $318 million. That is a lot of money being used to bribe choices instead of creating genuine compelling differentiation in the products or compelling differentiation in the marketing programs themselves.

Just so you don't scoff and consider me a naive theorist at this point, I will show you an example of how **Levi's** became the market leader in Japan through using an idea instead of payments to the trade. I will also show you, in the last section of this book, an example of how I created a new brand and seized market leadership in a category that typically does 81 percent of its volume at some kind of discounted price, does 100 percent of its volume on some form of extended-payment terms (another form of bribery), and takes an average of 38 percent of its volume back at the end of the season in returns—*and yet we did none of these things.*

Real marketing does not require bribery to succeed.

We achieved market leadership selling every single bottle at full price (no trade discounts), with no extended payment terms, and by accepting only 2 percent in returns. This brand, **Bullfrog** Amphibious Formula Sunblock, represents proof that the widespread practice of discounting can be circumvented. It just takes brand differentiation, genuine bravery, and a little patience.

Another brand we'll examine, **Bose** speaker systems, manages to do the same thing. Bose does not discount even at its own outlet stores. The fact is that it can be done. Unfortunately, very few companies and executives have the courage to even try.

Bribery is not real marketing. And here is the gospel truth in all of its wonder. The more real marketing you do, the less bribery is required.

If you do a great job of influencing and managing the Chain of Choice step by step along your particular spectrum, you win. If you do less than a great job of influencing and managing the Chain of Choice at any point along this spectrum, you and your brand will suffer to one degree or another.

The following case study is an excellent example of how a company can manage the Chain of Choice and go from a nothing brand to the market leader.

BRAND STUDY: Levi's in Japan

Levi's once had a 4 percent share of the blue-jeans market in Japan. (This was back around 1979, seven months after introduction.) And as you can imagine, they were not happy with that kind of limited market impact.

All market research showed that what Japanese consumers wanted more than anything else was to wear authentic American blue jeans. Levi's were authentic. Levi's were made in America. The two biggest brands in Japan, **Big John** and **Edison,** shared almost 70 percent of the market and both were Japanese-owned, but consumers there thought they were American jeans.

Even worse, the same research that showed that consumers were wrong in their perception of Levi's as less American demonstrated that the hundreds of salespeople in Japanese stores that carried blue jeans had the same wrong perception. Since research showed that salespeople affected 70 percent of the blue jeans decisions, these salespeople had to be convinced that Levi's were more American as well.

Remember the Chain of Choice. Levi's wanted to be the market leader in Japan. They needed to control the choices both of retail buyers and salespeople and of consumers. To accomplish this, they executed two key programs.

The consumer program was built around an advertising campaign to emphasize that Americans wore Levi's. They chose free footage of dead American celebrities wearing Levi's (people like James Dean and Marilyn Monroe) and created the campaign theme of "American Heroes Wear Levi's." This advertising began to build awareness of Levi's as the chosen American brand, both with consumers and to a certain degree among the retail salespeople who saw the advertising.

But the second program made the difference. Levi's brought every blue-jeans retail buyer and salesperson in Japan into Tokyo for one giant meeting at their expense. They told the whole story to each person in this captive audience, most of whom had never been wined or dined or treated as important by anyone. Levi's then gathered all of these buyers and salespeople together for one dramatic aerial shot of them arranged in a parking lot covered in denim fabric in a shape that replicated the Levi's Batwing logo, all shouting "Revi's."

This shot then became the closing shot for the "American Heroes Wear Levi's" advertising: every blue-jeans seller in Japan thrusting a fist in the air and shouting "Revi's." Variations of the ad were run locally, zooming in on the local salespeople. What brand do you think these salespeople who were now on TV started recommending? What brand did they consider truly American? What brand did Japanese consumers start buying and wearing?

Levi's went from a 4 percent share of the Japanese market to an 18 percent share within a year, then to eventual brand leadership.

It is rarely enough to influence just one part of the chain. It takes too long to make the right things happen at the end of the chain. Levi's had that perspective; using it, they became a Killer Brand in Japan.

Managing and Controlling Choice

So your job as a marketer is to manage choice, and to do it with as little bribery as possible. In fact, the degree to which you will be able to name your price will be a function of how well you perform against the three factors that will make the real difference in your success: which Focus you choose, how precisely Aligned you can be and stay, and how strong the Linkage is to your brand name. Levi's tried for years to gain share in Japan by promoting price. Finally, they tried the principles of Killer Branding and became number one without cutting price.

With the principle of *Focus*, you are trying to create a differentiated expectation for your brand that is so compelling that your target everywhere along the spectrum will choose your brand over others, regardless of price or the deal of the moment. What expectation will drive choice? Can I create it? Can I deliver it?

With *Alignment*, you are trying to make your brand's focus and differentiation so clear that no one along the spectrum will be confused about which brand to choose or why.

With *Linkage*, you are trying to ensure that your target will remember your brand accurately and remember specifically why they should make your brand their choice.

Let competitors try to buy the business. Your job is to own the business.

Remember, creating and building a Killer Brand is all about managing and controlling choice . . . along the entire spectrum, along the Chain of Choice.

This is what we mean by "success" in the definition of a Killer Brand. You must garner a disproportionate share of choices along the spectrum because each choice rings a little cash register. Your eventual success will be the total of all those little cash register rings . . . all the little choices made on behalf of your brand.

To create a Killer Brand you must control choice.

3

Understand Expectation, and How Your Marketplace Really Works

What do I mean when I tell you to know how your marketplace works? I mean that you need to understand to the greatest degree possible the following:

* What and who actually controls your marketplace
* Where they are along the Chain of Choice
* What they expect, and how they make choices and decisions based on those expectations

Every single time that anyone along the chain makes a choice, they make it based upon an expectation: "If I make this choice, what can I expect?" Sometimes their expectation will be what you tell them. Sometimes it will be the opposite. Sometimes they will create their own expectation based on perceptions of what you have done or what they can see. Sometimes it is based on their experiences, with you or with others. Sometimes it's even mysterious.

For example, consider a business-to-business marketplace for outsourced information technology. What expectation leads companies and the individuals in companies to decide that they need to outsource anything? What else specifically causes them to pursue an interest in outsourced technology? Is this really a company decision or are certain individuals leading the charge? If so, who are they? Why are they pulling the company in this direction?

In a consumer business, is the user the same as the buyer? Not always. Maybe Dad uses the toothpaste, but Mom is the one who buys it. Dad might specify the brand, or he might just use whatever is there. And the user-buyer categories might change over time.

In fact, the early history of a leading toothpaste brand provides an excellent example of how the subtleties of choice based on expectations can work.

BRAND STUDY: Who Buys the Toothpaste, and Why

Most of us remember the "Look, no cavities" **Crest** commercials with kids running into a scene all excited about their dental reports.

What you probably don't remember is that when this campaign started, the situation featured a child running into a room and shouting, "Look, Mom, no cavities." This advertising copy structure made sense if you realized that Mom picked and purchased the toothpaste that the child used.

This early campaign was successful, but nowhere near as successful as it became after market research revealed that Mom might have chosen the toothpaste, but Dad was more concerned with cavities. It is unclear whether his concern at the time was health-related or cost-related, but in those days before working Moms, Dads did tend to pay the dental bills.

At any rate, the campaign was changed to "Look, Dad, no cavities!" Mom became the heroine for choosing Crest, and sales began to soar. A side benefit of this change was that the targeted buyer, Mom, was glorified for her choice. Don't forget this point about glorifying the buyer. You will see the same principle in other examples in this book.

This is a great example of understanding a nuance—namely, that the bread is not always buttered by the person who eats it. And sometimes nuances affect expectations that in turn affect choices.

Qualitative Research

This chapter is not long enough to contain all of the principles and methods by which you learn how a category works. But understanding categories generally involves market research, both qualitative and quantitative, so let's talk a little about each kind of research, starting with the former.

Qualitative research consists of individualized discussions with people that probe their attitudes, decision-making, needs, wants, expectations, and so on. Such research is considered qualitative and not quantitative for two reasons: first, you talk with too few people to have a statistically reliable base, and, second, you often do not ask them the same questions in the same way. Rather, you strive to have an illuminating discussion with each person, discussions from which you can learn and develop hypotheses.

Qualitative research includes one-on-one interviews and/or focus groups with consumers, executives, buyers, nurses, or anyone else important in the Chain of Choice for your brand. You talk to them about ideas, discovering insights, improving ideas, etc. Qualitative research is not about measuring the potential impact of an idea or insight. You cannot make smart go-or-no-go decisions based on qualitative research. What you can do is listen to people and get ideas.

Some of the best ideas you will ever have will come from carefully listening to people talk about your business. You've seen this technique spoofed on TV, where someone sits behind a one-way mirror in the dark and listens to people being interviewed. But in the real world, such research can be a powerful tool for a good listener, one who knows how to categorize knowledge, form insights, and generate ideas.

Here, for example, is a marketing idea as it might have come from qualitative research.

Imagine that you are in a dark backroom behind one-way mirrors listening to a moderator interview a group of non–tea drinkers about why they don't drink tea.

The respondents have the usual assortment of reasons why they prefer other beverages, both hot and cold. Then someone makes an offhand comment. "When I think of tea, I think of little old ladies."

Sounds like a problem, doesn't it, if you want young people to drink tea. *Wrong.* This comment presents an opportunity.

This is an excellent example of listening well, garnering insight, and creating a big idea. For instance, this listening could have led to the advertising campaign featuring the slogan "Look at all those little old ladies drinkin' **Lipton** tea."

The advertising, as you may recall, featured young women, teenagers, young men—virtually everyone *but* "little old ladies"—drinking Lipton tea. And it was part of a number of marketing activities that accelerated and broadened tea consumption in the United States.

BRAND STUDY: The Bunny Versus the CopperTop

Qualitative research also allows you to dig deep. The following example from the battery business shows how.

Both **Energizer** and **Duracell** are alkaline batteries with no technical differences in performance. Most people know that. Most people agree. But do they really believe it?

We once conducted one-on-one interviews with battery users. They would state that either brand was equal. Then the interviewer would pull out a $5 bill, and ask the following question, "These two brands are either exactly equal or they aren't. If you can answer correctly whether they are equal or not, I will give you this $5 bill." About 90 percent of respondents then answered that they were probably different after all, not equal. And thus earned the $5 bill.

The interviewer then pulled out another $5 bill and said, "Yes, they are not equal. One brand lasts longer than the other does. If you can correctly guess which one, I will give you another $5 bill."

Almost everyone guessed Duracell even though the technology was exactly the same. Why?

Further probing suggested that these expectations were most likely caused by Duracell's "**CopperTop**" advertising and but even more by the fact that Energizer at that time was sometimes confused with the **Eveready** flashlight batteries that did not last very long. The names Energizer and Eveready sounded similar. They were both owned by the same company. And the packaging was black and silver on both Energizer and Eveready.

Duracell, on the other hand, had never put its name or similar colors or package design on anything other than an alkaline battery, so none of the Duracell brand keys were ever incorrectly associated with or linked to plain flashlight battery failures. Qualitative research suggested the theory that the perception of superior battery performance (durability) was more related to lack of remembered failure than to actual battery performance or experienced durability. Consumers did not remember how long a battery lasted unless it gave out too early and did not meet their expectations. They remembered when it did not last.

Was this in-depth learning about user expectations worth giving 100 or so people an extra $10 for their real feelings? You bet it was.

This particular piece of research (about $100,000 at the time) was the first step in a progressive learning program that led eventually to the creation of the Energizer Bunny, to the de-emphasis of the carbon flashlight battery business by Eveready, and then to the eventual change in the name of the company from Eveready to the Energizer Company.

You should realize that qualitative research is tricky. In my experience it is misused over 75 percent of the time by people who use it to make decisions rather than to generate insight and ideas. If you are interested in learning how to properly use qualitative research, I recommend you read an excellent book by Tom Greenbaum (a friend of mine) that is titled *The Handbook for Focus Group Research*.

Quantitative Research

The other kind of market research is *quantitative research*. This is used to "quantify," to count the percentage of people who think or feel a particular way. You may get a wonderful idea out of qualitative research, then expose it to a statistically representative sample of consumers and find out that only 2 percent of them like it. You just happened to have a few of those 2 percent in your focus groups.

Quantitative research means asking the exact same questions in the exact same way and in exact same order to a statistically representative base of people. You can conduct this kind of research with personal interviews, over the phone, in the mail, or on the Internet. It requires no customized interaction on the part of the interviewer. Quantitative bases can be as small as 125, but are generally larger (600+) to allow for splitting the base after the research into meaningful subgroups for analysis—e.g., young versus old, men versus women, users versus nonusers.

Quantitative research includes custom research as well as all kinds of syndicated data, such as Nielsen data and MRI data. One of my favorite examples concerns **Visine** for eyes.

Visine was a relatively small brand marketed for relief of dry, itchy eyes. Users complained that air conditioning, allergies, and dry air caused their eyes to have problems.

Late one night at Benton & Bowles, the Visine advertising agency at the time, a media buyer was poring over reams of data on users and usage. She happened to also work on the **Jack Daniels** bourbon account. All of a sudden she was overcome with a wave of lateral thinking and noticed that the demographics and psychographics of heavy Visine users matched up exactly with the demographics and psychographics of the heavy bourbon drinker.

Based on this quantitative finding, she hypothesized that the brand was being driven by morning-after usage among heavy drinkers. Additional analysis supported that hypothesis, but the brand management team did not want to reposition the brand overtly to heavy drinkers, so the idea of "Gets the Red Out" was born to accomplish the task.

Visine sales grew over 400 percent over the next few years. All this growth traces to a tiny little discovery in a set of quantitative data that happened to be noticed by a giant of a marketing person.

Political polling is quantitative. Quantitative means that you count the number of people who have a particular attitude, give the same feedback, have the same interests, etc.

And sometimes you do not have to conduct a custom research study to derive a brilliant analysis. You can do the same with syndicated data, and a large statistically reliable database.

Which is more important, qualitative or quantitative research? Actually, it generally takes both kinds of research learning to understand and validate how individuals along a Chain of Choice make their decisions and what expectations motivate them. One day I may write a whole book about how to use qualitative and quantitative research, but that's not our focus here, so let's go on to the power of expectation.

31

BRAND STUDY: Who Deodorizes Their Carpet?

In attempting to understand the driving expectation or need that caused users of carpet deodorizes to spray their carpets before vacuuming, one of our consultants working for Arm & Hammer noticed that sales of carpet deodorizers happened to skew toward households that owned pets. The skew was substantial but never noticed in the stacks of data that had always been available. Pet owners were over eight times as likely to use the category as non–pet owners.

Arm & Hammer used this discovery to develop a new fragrance that they called **Pet Fresh**, developed specifically to control odors from dogs and cats. Pet Fresh became quickly the number one item in the category, and helped propel Arm & Hammer to the leadership position in the category. Out of that finding, Arm & Hammer began to understand how important odor control was to pet owners, particularly those with indoor dogs and cats.

Today Arm & Hammer has a $200 million business surrounding the control of dog and cat odors.

Embrace the Power of Expectation

Think about the last time you were disappointed. What happened?

You made a choice based on an expectation and your expectation was not realized. This is a simple, yet profound concept. You made a choice based upon an expectation, and your expectation was not fulfilled. Thus you were disappointed.

Nothing is as powerful to a brand marketer as *Expectation*. All choices are made based on expectations, even subliminal choices.

In the example given earlier, people chose Duracell when it came right down to it because they did not expect it to fail, and deep down somewhere in the recesses of their memory, they were concerned that Energizer might fail. This expectation was to the benefit of Duracell, and to the detriment of Energizer.

Do consumers always expect differences? Absolutely not. Sometimes they expect two choices to be the same, to be interchangeable. When they don't expect differences, price kicks in. What's more, when they expect differences that are not important enough to compel their choice, price can kick in again.

So absolutely, unequivocally, your job is to **create a compelling and differentiating expectation for your brand**, or you will never have a chance to enjoy the benefits of owning a Killer Brand.

CHOOSING "I DON'T CARE"

Back when pay phones were still common, but after deregulation, there existed a moment when a telephone operator would ask you what carrier you wished to use for a long-distance call. Many phone users expected the exact same service no matter which carrier they used.

An enterprising entrepreneur in Dallas, Texas, registered brand names for long-distance service such as "I Don't Care," "Anyone's Okay," "It Doesn't Matter," "I Don't Give a Damn," and several others. He had a computer in his bedroom from which he could route calls.

When an operator asked a caller which carrier they wanted to use, and a caller responded, "I don't care," the call was routed through his long-distance brand.

Because none of the big-time long-distance brands had yet established differentiated and compelling expectations for their brands, this enterprising young man made almost $100 million in his first twelve months based on consumer ennui.

Is expectation a powerful concept? Absolutely.

Create the right expectation for your brand, and you have a foundation for success. Without it, everything is going to be difficult. Let's consider the following case study of a brand that made the most of the expectations associated with it.

BRAND STUDY: A Product Famous for What It's Not

When **Neutrogena** decided to expand the brand's core expectation beyond skin care and into the hair care business, they started with such a foundation for success.

Neutrogena was more famous for what it wasn't than for what it was. The core expectation was "neutral to the skin" (the exact translation of "Neutrogena," by the way). It was famous for purity and what was not in it. That's why Neutrogena soap was clear. Years of reading a print ad headline through the actual bar of soap had built this perception of purity among millions of women.

When it came to expanding this idea into hair care, the late Mike Stark, then with a new products consulting and development company in Kansas City, proposed a revolutionary idea. He knew from other work in hair care that many women were unsatisfied with their hair, and that many of them blamed the shampoo they were using and as a result switched shampoos every six months or so.

Mike proposed that Neutrogena shampoo be the shampoo to use for a couple of weeks when you were switching from one shampoo brand to another. Neutrogena was so pure and so free of the extra ingredients in other shampoos that it would help get your hair back to normal so you could try something else.

This is a perfect example of brilliantly harnessing an expectation. Women blamed shampoos if they did not like the way their hair looked.

Neutrogena was an unusual brand in that it was famous for what it was not, rather than for what it was.

Neutrogena shampoo was thus introduced with the idea that the buyer could "use it to get your hair back to normal between switching shampoos." The shampoo itself was clear, of course, just like the soap. What's more, it was premium priced (over a dollar an ounce in 1980), which aligned to pure, expensive ingredients.

With less than $2 million in print advertising among category spending of over $300 million a year in advertising, and by telling women to use it for only two weeks, Neutrogena shampoo became one of the largest single shampoos in the category, with almost $50 million in sales in the first year.

Women did not expect Neutrogena to make their hair look better, merely to help get it back to normal so they could try something else. And that resonated with enough of them to drive a Killer Brand result.

Since then, Neutrogena has improved on that idea, and now recommends that you use their shampoo for a week every six weeks or so to remove residues and get your hair back to normal so you will not have to switch shampoos unless you want to.

Success Comes from Individual Choices Based on Individual Expectations

In the Levi's example given earlier, what expectation drove consumer choice? The brand that was considered more American was the one chosen. What expectation drove retail salespeople's choice of what to recommend? The brand that would be easier to sell because it was more American was the one chosen.

These are not exactly the same expectation. For one of them, "more American" is the expectation. For the other, "more American" is the reason to believe the more compelling expectation of "easier or better to sell."

This is not a meaningless nuance. You need to understand what expectation drives choice on behalf of your brand for every key link along your Chain of Choice. Here is a suggestion for navigating this minefield of "expectations" that will determine your success or failure.

Isolate the Key Links

Along your Chain of Choice, which links are the most critical to your success? For instance, in the carpeting business, the retail salesperson controls over 80 percent of consumer choices. In the eye-care business, the eye-care professional determines from 30 percent to 90 percent of choices for contact lenses and lens-care products, depending on the individual category. In the choice of a college by a graduating high-school senior, the high-school counselor is often a key person, particularly in debunking a choice. With computer devices and software, word of mouth from early users and opinions from magazine editors are key; with floor cleaners, no editor is interested, nor is any reader going to review sources to learn. Every category is different.

But one thing is common to every category. You cannot manage everyone. It's too much work and too much of an investment. So, like a military strategist, you have to decide where to focus your efforts and forces. There will always be key links whose actions not only are more important to your brand but also tend to influence the actions of other links.

Figure out who they are.

Become Behavioral

For each targeted link, become behavioral. What exactly is it that you want each link to do for your brand? Spell out the individual behavior in writing. This is a very important step because it orients your thinking toward producing the correct action on behalf of your brand.

Determine the Motivating Expectation for Each

Determine what each targeted link in the Chain of Choice expects from your brand—what will make each link respond as you desire. Use market research, do your own interviewing, whatever you can afford, but do a good job. Spend the time necessary to get it right. If you get the wrong results, you will have saved neither a cent nor a minute of time.

Deliver the Expectation

This is self-explanatory. If a physician wants to see superiority proven by clinical results in order to recommend your new drug, do the clinical research. If a mother wants to know that your gelatin dessert is better for her children than **Jell-O**, create the product, the story, and the evidence. If a grocery store buyer wants to know that your brand will accelerate category sales, create the evidence, don't just make the claim.

One way to really understand is to take each key link in the chain and, in your mind, *become* the link. Become the sales person. What expectation would motivate you? Become the trade buyer. What expectation would motivate you? Become the consumer. What motivation would motivate you? I remember in the beginnings of my consulting career how we followed this exact policy. Someone in our organization had to become a user no matter what we were working on. We drew straws to see which of us had to start having injections of collagen when we were working with the Collagen Corporation back in the earliest days of plastic surgery by injection. Thankfully I did not get the winning straw! But one of us did, and he started the therapy. The extra insight we received from his experiences and feelings made the difference in our ability to really understand the consumer.

THE FIRST STEP: KILLER FOCUS

4

Find a Killer Focus

Almost everyone in business will agree that having a strong focus is good. Why is it, then, that so few people actually practice focus?

Perhaps they have all agreed with and bought into a principle that they don't really understand.

When it comes to creating a Killer Brand, the first principle of **Focus** asserts that no matter how many strong selling points or expectations might exist for your brand, you are better off choosing one and making it the sole focus of your brand.

For instance, if your brand has three very strong and compelling differences, any one of which could be the expectation used to control choice, you are better off choosing one of them and making it the sole focus of your brand than trying to communicate all three.

There is no use talking about what kind of focus is best and how you go about developing and choosing the best focus until you agree that the whole idea of Focus is actually important. Lack of focus is the most common failing of brands and people in the business of branding—having no focus, trying to focus on multiple benefits, distracting from focus by adding secondary benefits.

You are better off having a focus that is not the best, rather than no focus at all.

This declaration is a good one to nail to the back of your retina. Virtually any focus is better than no focus. No matter what, you are not going to choose to focus on an expectation so wrong that it is compelling to no one.

BRAND STUDY: Playing the Bud Bowl

The **Bud** Bowl is generally considered the most successful promotion in the history of the beer business. I have worked for both **Miller** and **Coors**. I even drink beer, although only occasionally. During the entire ten-year reign of Bud Bowl, I never really understood what the promotion was or what was in it for me the Beer Drinker.

But everyone at Anheuser-Busch seemed to understand. They mobilized their prodigious, category-leading sales force and distribution system and made Bud Bowl succeed beyond their wildest dreams.

Bud Bowl was created in 1989 as a special advertising campaign to increase retail interest to beer in January, the slowest-selling beer season of the year. It featured a football game between Bud bottles and Bud Light bottles. Real NFL players were hired as the voices for the bottles in the commercials. Real NFL announcers did the play-by-play. Each year there was a score for the game. Later on, other Bud products like Bud Dry and Bud Ice were allowed to field teams.

Bud Bowl was different and crazy and out of the mold. But it did relate to January and to the buildup to the Super Bowl, which was rapidly becoming the largest single event for in-home entertaining, even bigger than Thanksgiving and Christmas.

And dealers built displays of Budweiser products to support the commercials. And those displays sold beer that otherwise would not have been sold and consumed in January.

But there was no brilliant idea here. Research showed that consumers had not an inkling of what the idea was. It never converted to a compelling promotion to beer drinkers. But it was compelling to dealers along the Chain of Choice and thus worked to build Bud sales.

The fact that the company itself focused so solidly behind this concept with advertising, sales support, and dealer incentives proves that focus itself can work even if the idea itself is not powerful.

Choosing a Date

Let's use another example of choice outside of typical brand marketing—choosing a date—because it will show how tempting lack of focus can be, or how tempting the lure of multiple-focus can be. After all, how can you choose one point of focus when in fact, not every prospect will be interested in that particular point?

The answer is that you have to give up trying to sell all prospects, and make sure that you sell at least one of them. This is the raw power of focus. Choose the right focus and sell a lot of them. Accept that **you will never sell to all of them.**

Let's complete an exercise together. This example features a female prospect looking for Mr. Right. Assume you are the female. I specifically tell you about six different male candidates to whom I could introduce you. But I will introduce you to only one. I give you three good reasons why each is different and why you should like them, or prefer one to the other five.

(If you are a male, by the way, stay right with me. Just reverse the gender in the example. Or put yourself on the marketing side rather than the prospect side. Assume that you are one of the males in these choice matrixes. By the way, there are many parallels between effective courting and effective marketing.)

Here goes:

Jack, Bob, Mike, Rudy, Jim, and Rob. Six brand choices among many men. Just for kicks, which of the choices do you already remember more readily without knowing anything more than their names? Jack, Bob, Mike, Rudy, Jim or Rob? If you said Rudy, you will be among the majority. Why? Because the name itself is differentiated, and thus easier to remember among a group of Bobs and Robs. We will come back to that later.

Here is what I want you to remember about each of the six choices.

* Jack is divorced, loves kids, and plays polo.
* Bob is single, works in finance, and makes a lot of money.
* Mike is very fit, once played pro football, and is a real estate agent.
* Rudy is kind, sensitive, and also a real estate agent.
* Jim is divorced, loves golf, and wants to have kids.
* Rob makes a lot of money, loves women, and is difficult to tie down.

Now, after one reading of this list, put the book down for a second before you continuing reading.

Don't look back at the list. Remember what you can about the six choices. I am going to set you up with a date with one of them, but you can only choose one. What do you remember? How do you make your choice?

If you find it difficult to remember clearly who is who and what is different about them, you are in the majority. You have too much information.

Now let's consider another list of six: Roy, Wilson, Max, Philippe, Josh, and Pete.

I will give you one focused point on each. Here goes:

* Roy is rich.
* Wilson is a jazz musician.
* Max paints nudes.
* Philippe owns a vineyard.
* Josh is a world traveler.
* Pete is hard to tie down.

Now put the book down again for a second, and remember what you can.

Back already? Once again, I will set you up on a date with one of these men. What do you remember? Whom do you choose?

Can you remember more information about the six choices? Even though you were given less information? You should be able to.

Further, the specific choice in the preceding list that is differentiated in the way that most interests you is the choice that you are most likely to remember. If you love wine more than jazz or art, you are most likely to remember that one of the choices that you were given owns a vineyard even if you don't remember his name. If you like to travel the world, you are most likely to remember that one of the choices is a world traveler.

We can remember one thing about a choice more readily than we can remember many things. You can take this one principle to the bank.

The less information we are given, the more likely we are to remember it.

The Graduation Speech

If you are reading this book, you probably were graduated from some educational institution. Think back to your graduation exercises. Who gave the speech? What did they say?

I cannot remember any of this information for any of my graduations. I don't know who spoke at my high school or my university commencement. Can you remember yours?

But what if you and I had graduated in the UK, and Winston Churchill had given the address? It would be easy enough to remember that the great Winston Churchill was our commencement speaker. But would we remember what he said? I believe we would.

Churchill did give a memorable commencement address. It was a big deal, and a plethora of world journalists were there to cover the event. All were set to make copious notes.

When introduced, Churchill walked up to the podium, settled himself, cleared his throat, looked over the vast audience, began and ended with "Never, never, never give up," and walked off the stage.

Would you remember that graduation advice the rest of your life? Is that focus or what?

What is more remarkable is that this speech is quoted broadly, and attributed to Oxford as well as the prep academy that Churchill attended. You can find hundreds of examples of it on the Internet. But it is very possible that this speech never even existed. There is much argument.

So here we have a commencement speech that is remembered for its simplicity and focus, even though it may never have been given at all.

How is that as an example of the power of focus?

Here's another example of the importance of focus. I want you to remember just five points from this book: the roles of **Choice** and **Expectation**, and the brand principles of **Focus, Alignment,** and **Linkage.**

Would they be easier to remember if there were a list of eleven or thirteen?

It is simple. It is much easier to remember one thing about a choice than several things about a choice. And no matter what your brand is, your prospect will give it less attention than you do. You can go to the bank on this also. No one pays attention to your business like you do. No one. And they never will.

The Power of Focus

So for starters, **Focus** itself is fundamental to Killer Branding.

Does that mean that you pay attention to nothing else about your brand offering? Absolutely not. As you will see in the chapters on Alignment, you will care about everything. In Killer Branding, nothing is left to chance.

But you do focus on a single compelling and differentiating expectation. You do build the brand and all brand communications around that focused expectation. And then you concentrate on delivering that focused expectation.

In your real world you will hear Focus referred to as many different things. You will hear "promise," "benefit," "attribute," "USP (Unique Selling Proposition)." In my company, we work smarter and are more successful by thinking in terms of "expectation," but any one of these similar terms is fine just as long as you understand and define it correctly. As I mentioned earlier, this change to thinking about "expectation" has helped us immensely, particularly me personally.

BRAND STUDY: A Big Success with Tiny Houses

In 1997, Jay Shafer, an architect specializing in sustainable environments and urban planning, designed, built, and moved into a 100-square-foot house. He liked minimalist living so much that he built himself an even smaller house—70 square feet—and sold the first one.

How much demand can there be for houses smaller than most people's bathrooms? Not much, but **Tumbleweed Tiny House Company** is a real testimony to focus.

Jay has created a sustainable brand from this focus. He has numerous plans you can buy and also does custom designs for people who want to live in minimum space. What is the expectation? The answer is, "The room you need and not an inch more." These are my words, not Jay's. And apparently, about 100 square feet is all that we need.

If you think about it, plenty of our ancestors probably lived in caves that were smaller, and survived and prospered enough to give birth to and raise the next generation that eventually led to you and me. And in developing countries, a Tumbleweed Tiny House would be considered a luxury by most.

And there are enough people in the United States who resonate to this expectation, for either a primary house or an escape cabin somewhere, that Jay Shafer has a legitimate brand going.

If Jay were to start selling add-on wings and such, he would eventually lose his focus, but for now he is spot on it, and is succeeding with an idea that most of us would consider ridiculous and irrelevant to our needs.

This is the power of focus.

The meaning of focus is just that—single-minded devotion to one principal expectation. And fortunately for you, you won't find a lot of competitors dedicated to focus. It is too difficult for most people to focus. The temptation to wander off focus is just too great.

BRAND STUDY: Crest Fallen

Remember the earlier story of Crest's zoom to leadership? It was a leadership that lasted a long time.

"Fighting cavities was the whole idea behind Crest." These were Crest's words, not mine. Unfortunately, Crest lost its focus, and began to introduce anti-plaque line extensions, and whitening extensions, and flavors, and toothbrushes. The overall business is larger now, but Crest is no longer the market leader in toothpaste, having gone from a position of over 40 percent market share to under 25 percent.

Private sources within Procter & Gamble also tell me that the profit ratio on Crest is down by a third, something that happens to Killer Brands when they lose their focus.

I cannot tell you that the second will always follow from the first, but I cannot find a single example of a Killer Brand losing its focus and not reducing its profitability (ratio of profits to sales, not the total amount of profits). If any reader knows of one, please e-mail me about it at *flane@franklaneltd.com*.

Let's examine this for a moment. The challenges to the brand's focus were considerable. Cavities began to go away as a prime concern and as a reality. Fluoridated water, fluoride treatments from dentists, and even Crest itself combined to largely eliminate cavities as a primary oral concern. The expectation for cavity control became less compelling to toothpaste buyers and users.

Rather than find another compelling focus toward which to migrate or to leap, Crest chose to pursue multiple focuses.

The Chinese proverb "He who chases two rabbits catches neither" surged into play, and now Crest (at least for the moment) has lost its leadership and perhaps its momentum. It will be interesting to watch how the battle for the $10 billion oral care market plays itself out over the next decade.

Focus on a Compelling Expectation

Remember that your job is to control choices. Every single choice is based on an expectation. With no expectation for your brand, you are not in the running. With an expectation for your brand that is not important enough or is insufficiently compelling, you do not get chosen. Worse yet, if you have an expectation for your brand that is off-putting, you are completely out of the hunt.

So **your brand must represent an expectation** or you are not in the game at all, and if you want more than your fair share of choices, your brand's expectation must compel a disproportionate share of targets along the entire Chain of Choice to choose your brand.

I have a good friend and associate, Jim Taylor, who is one of the world's more brilliant people. He is a futurist, an author, and a successful marketer. Before he entered the realm of marketing he was head of the Department of Rhetoric (classic art of persuasion) at the University of California at Berkeley. I think Jim may be actually too smart for his own good.

Jim and I spent years arguing whether it is better for a brand to focus on an important benefit (but not be so differentiated) or to focus on a differentiated benefit (but perhaps not such an important one). *Note:* We both believed in focus. We were just not so sure on what.

About ten years ago, he and I concluded that compelling was more important than differentiated and not compelling. When you cannot be both compelling and differentiated, a compelling focus delivered or talked about in a differentiated way was the second best position. The following brand story is an excellent example.

BRAND STUDY: Please Don't Squeeze the Charmin

Toilet tissue is like most categories in that one or two benefits (or expectations) are much more important than any other secondary benefits. You will run into this a lot.

In toilet tissue, softness is the most important expectation among over 40 percent of buyers and users. The second most important expectation is wet strength at 19 percent.

It takes close to a 30 percent share to be the market leader. You want to be the market leader. Do you have any choice but to focus on softness? Nothing else is important enough to enough users to drive market share. But four other brands already focus on softness. What to do?

Focus on softness in a different way.

That's what **Charmin** did. They made their softness irresistible—in fact, so irresistible that they appointed a brand spokesperson, Mr. Whipple, to guard Charmin in the store from shoppers who could not resist squeezing it. And they focused . . . on irresistible softness, in their advertising, on the display pieces, on the packaging, in their materials to the trade, and in their product.

For years Charmin was in reality *the* softest brand of toilet tissue. They utilized a patented technology for vacuuming water out of the tissue as it progressed through the manufacturing line rather than squeezing it out. This produced a tissue that was softer, fluffier, and airier than other tissues.

Charmin used this focus on softness and Mr. Whipple to maintain market leadership for thirty years, even though other brands also focused on softness. Charmin found a way to differentiate softness.

Now that Dick Williams, the actor who played Mr. Whipple is not around any more, Charmin is still selling softness, albeit in a less differentiated way, at least in my opinion. And the patent has expired.

Focus is tough to sustain, but it's good to have for as long as you can.

Keep the Focus Up Front

In my career I have found numerous examples like the following when a brand has its focus but buries it so that only they know. This is a shame, but if you're not careful it may be true for your business as well.

Nebraska

I was sitting on an airplane reading one of the airline magazines a number of years ago and happened to read a small space ad for the State of Nebraska. I don't remember what the headline was, or how the ad copy began or ended. But I do remember one sentence in the copy. I believe this sentence should have been the headline and focus of the pitch. It was differentiated, compelling to the appropriate target audience, relevant enough to be very believable.

"Nebraska is what America used to be."

In this case, as Albert Brooks said to Holly Hunter in the movie *Broadcast News*, they buried the lead. Nebraska's being what America used to be is the big idea here.

If I had anything to do with the decision for Nebraska, I would focus on this idea and make it more and more true and more and more memorable. Like attracts like, and to the degree such a campaign might successfully attract new companies and residents to the state, they would probably add to the concept rather than detract from it. Why would this focused expectation attract your choice if you were not already interested in moving back a little to a gentler time?

Viagra

Then occasionally you happen upon a killer expectation, a focus so powerful that you don't have to do much else.

How compelling can an expectation be? Think of the emergence and rapid growth of **Viagra.**

Viagra is an interesting mistake. The project started out as compound UK-92,480 for the treatment of angina. It seemed to produce the intended effects until human trials when the potential drug fell too short of expectation to be introduced. However, scientists at Pfizer noticed an interesting side effect that will go down in history as one of the most profitable mistakes in the history of business.

Viagra was subsequently introduced for the treatment of erectile dysfunction, the interesting side effect noticed. Brand sales zoomed at $10 per tablet. Remember how in an earlier chapter we talked about naming your price if your compelling differentiation was strong enough? The expectation in Viagra was strong enough to a sufficient number of men even at $10 per tablet to drive the brand to $1 billion in its first year of marketing.

There is a large dose of truth in the Viagra expectation, but testing and real consumer usage show that the brand expectation is met far less consistently than most consumer brands that are never introduced because they are not good enough. That is because sometimes a target audience wants their expectation to be true so badly that they will overlook product failure.

You have probably witnessed this same phenomenon with the **Windows** operating system from Microsoft. You've seen the comparison of Windows to automobiles, and realize that you would not tolerate the vagaries and failures in Windows if it were an automobile. But the expectation is so compelling, "hassle-free computer operations," that you want it to be true, and millions of computer users around the world still use Windows instead of **Apple** or **Linux,** both of which are far more hassle-free.

Charmin demonstrates a good example of differentiating a compelling but otherwise generic expectation. Nebraska is a good example of missing the big idea or compelling expectation in your product. (This happens more often than you think.) Viagra is a good example of discovering an expectation in your product that is far more compelling than what you set out to create.

Roundup

Another example of unexpected consequences was **Roundup,** which was developed originally by Monsanto as a rust remover for metal fencing, particularly barbed wire around cattle pastures.

During product-use tests, the technical team realized that everywhere that the formula dripped to the ground, every living plant died. Quickly the company realized that the market for a general purpose herbicide was much larger than a metal fence rust remover, and the formula was relaunched as Roundup.

Monsanto (which was at that time headed up by a Procter & Gamble–trained, marketing-oriented CEO) thought Roundup was such a powerful idea that they sampled American farms with enough product to treat an acre. After the brand was firmly established on farms, it was expanded into the residential market and is now a clear market leader, a true Killer Brand.

If you get lucky and you can focus on an expectation that is both sufficiently compelling and differentiating, you can move on to Alignment. But most of the time you will focus on an expectation that is compelling but fairly common in the category like the Charmin example. Then you will have to find a way to differentiate your focus just as they had to.

5

Differentiate Your Focus

A focus on a compelling expectation will generally not be enough to create a Killer Brand. Your brand expectation needs to be compelling and differentiated from other brands that offer the same or a similar expectation.

You may be one of the lucky few. Your brand expectation may already be differentiated. But if you stay in the business long enough, sooner or later you will not be so lucky and will need to work diligently to differentiate your brand. And it is quantum times more difficult to find a compelling differentiation than it is to just focus on compelling. So you should learn now and learn well.

All businesses have two choices. Either you can choose to be differentiated and market yourself as a brand, or you can choose to be me-too and market yourself as a commodity.

Aristotle on Brand Differentiation

In our quest to develop a Killer Brand, what can we learn from Aristotle? Aristotle taught that all things in relationship to one another are either the same or they are different. No two things can be both the same and different.

Further, he taught that among things that are different from one another, there are only two kinds of differences: differences in *kind* and differences in *degree*. He also distinguished between real differences and perceived differences.

If you have a shovel and a rake, you have a difference in kind. If you have a small shovel and a big shovel, then you have a difference in degree. If you have a silver-colored shovel and a rusty shovel, you have a difference in kind when comparing the colors and a difference in degree when perceiving their relative age. However, you can perceive the rusty shovel to be older than the silver shovel, and it may not be true. It is only your perception.

When you perceive one to be silver and the other to be rusty, it is a true difference in kind because the proof of the different color is in the seeing.

You cannot, however, see the difference in age; you can only infer it. Thus it is perceived, and can be real or not real.

Brand Relevance

As pointed out in the Aristotelian discussion above, brands can be different in kind or in degree, or they can be the same. These differences may be either real or perceived.

If customers do not perceive a difference in kind or degree, then—no matter what internal company folklore claims—to them, you are the same. This is a key point. If customers do not see the difference, you are the same (whether there is a real difference or not). No see = Me too!

For instance, the difference between **Folgers** and **Maxwell House** may be perceived by some customers. They have both worked to produce a difference in the minds of coffee drinkers.

But the reality is that they are very, very similar, and not every consumer perceives a difference. To those who don't perceive the difference, Folgers and Maxell House are the same, just two very large me-toos.

However, along comes **Starbucks.** The difference between Starbucks and Maxwell House coffee is a difference in kind and in degree. The difference in kind might be the experience of drinking it, or the source of the beans, etc. The difference in degree would be its relative strength, strong coffee versus weak coffee, etc.

Experience teaches us that a difference in kind is inherently better than a difference in degree (given, of course, that both are equally compelling).

> *The difference in kind between products is more powerful than a difference in degree.*

Differences in kind are more difficult to compete with, and less likely to be leapfrogged in the short term. For example, Windows represented a difference in kind from MS-DOS and OS2. It was difficult to create an operating system to adequately compete with Windows. In what way should a competitor be different?

Differences in degree tend to be time-doomed, merely waiting for a competitive advance. For example, a 14.4 kbps modem is a difference in degree from a 9600 baud-rate modem, but it is easily leapfrogged by a 28.8 kbps, which in turn was leapfrogged by the next improvement in speed. In sunscreens, SPF 15 was leapfrogged by SPF 18, and now you can buy SPF 45, something that virtually anyone with extreme sun sensitivity needs.

Testing Brand Differences

Differences in kind can be tested and measured monadically—that is, testing and measuring the product all by itself. Try it, and use it. Tell me what you think. Compare it to your regular brand. Differences in kind do not have to be measured monadically, but they can be.

Differences in degree should always be tested and measured competitively—e.g., side-by-side, or paired comparison, or sequential monadic.

Real differences should be tested blind with no brand name or distinguishing packaging. You need to know if the difference is really there.

Perceived differences, on the other hand, can be and often should be tested within the contest of the expected perception. For instance, use a concept statement or a promise or an expectation. Put the perception in the tester's mind, and see if they agree after usage.

When you are dealing with differences in degree, one of the nuances is that "better" is a comparative term and can refer to one specific competitor, or to several, or even to your previous formula. If your strategy is to be merely "better," you need only test and measure against the brands versus which you intend to be better.

"Superior," however, is a superlative term and means the best— better than all other choices. A brand strategy of superiority requires careful and regular testing of all competitive choices.

If your stated mission is superior products (differences in degree), you must test the competitors' products. How can you know that you are superior to something that you have never tested?

Price

And there is one difference in degree—price—that is particularly tricky. I know I said that price was not one of the principles of Killer Branding—and it isn't—but price is almost always related to perception. While it is not a principle, it is nonetheless an important factor in differentiation.

One brand can be priced lower than another, but this cannot be a motivating difference in degree unless all other variables are the same. Thus, a lower price does you no good unless all other variables affecting the choice of your brand are judged to be at least equal.

A lower price only represents value on the same product or on one judged to be just as desirable, if not more so. That's why a high-priced brand on sale is so motivating.

A lower price on a choice judged to be less desirable is not automatically a value. For example, a private-label product is only of value to a consumer who thinks the product is just as good. A lower price on a choice judged to be less desirable represents a trade-off. Trade-offs introduce the potential for comparative confusion.

Confusion requires consumers to think. Causing the customer to think is never in your best interest. Let's repeat that: Causing the customer to think is *never* in your best interest. Make choices so clear that a customer does not need to think. They need only to act.

The customer, consumer, trade, or business buyer spends less energy thinking about your brand and relative choices than you do. Your job is to do the thinking for him, and make his choice clear.

And that brings us to the worst facet of price as a differentiator, the introduction of doubt. Lower price causes the customer to doubt or question other variables. Introducing doubt is not in your best interest either.

If your brand does not represent a real difference in kind, or a real difference in degree, then it is a me-too product. Any difference that becomes meaningful for this kind of brand must be produced in the consumer's perception—by you and your actions.

If your brand does not represent a motivating difference in kind, or a motivating difference in degree, it behaves as a me-too product. You have the same job to do. A difference that might be motivating and compelling must be created in the consumer's perception.

A real difference that exists but is not perceived has no value. The best alternative is a perceived difference with a foundation in reality.

The lesson from Aristotle is clear. Build into your product a real and motivating difference in kind, or a real and motivating difference in degree. If you cannot, you must create one in the consumer's perception. Otherwise, you are the same, and will be left to compete solely on the basis of price or temporary promotion. Sound familiar?

Is your brand expectation the same as or different than other brands'? Is your brand a difference in kind (Spanx, for example), or a difference in degree (Duracell, for example)?

Can your brand focus be differentiated or must you focus on the same expectation that the rest of the category does and find a way to differentiate a nondifferentiated focus?

Competitive Set Worksheet

Go get a blank sheet of paper. Actually, get several blank sheets of paper. Let's do an exercise together and wrestle with these issues within one category. How about cars?

How many potential differentiators exist in the automobile category? Using a separate piece of paper for each characteristic, write down the qualities upon which a buyer might rate a car and possibly be compelled to choose, such as Design, Fuel Economy, Safety, Reliability, Durability, Driving Fun, Speed, etc.

Next, list the car brands that you consider to be differentiated from others under each characteristic, whether the brand chooses to focus on that characteristic or not. Then determine whether each brand as differentiated on your lists represents a difference in kind or a difference in degree.

For example, a Mini Cooper is differentiated on design because no other car brand looks anything like it. That design difference is a difference in kind. The Mini Cooper is also differentiated on size, but that difference is a difference in degree.

Here is what this exercise should demonstrate:

1. You will find it difficult to construct this competitive set. Why? Because in the absence of research that you do not have, it will be difficult to list every possible differentiator and impossible to know quantitatively how many car buyers

think which one is the most important. But some form of this is what each car buyer must do for herself before she begins to visit dealers. So the exercise will be good for you to complete as both a consumer and as a marketer.

2. It will serve to confirm how many possible variables and ideas exist in categories when it comes to deciding how to differentiate a brand.

3. You will be stunned at how many car brands are not differentiated and do not fit on your matrix at all. (As an aside, you will see those brands discount-priced the most and to the greatest degree.)

4. You will begin to be able to fit your perceptions of a car brand with what it says about itself, and see that some differentiations are self-evident and others have to be communicated. For instance, you cannot look at a BMW and know that it is fun to drive. You cannot look at a Mercedes and know that it is built on superior engineering. Each case requires communication.

Complete the exercise even if you have to think about it over several days. Trust me. You will think of other differentiators after you complete your first draft, but keep at it. You will also remember other cars that fit into certain differentiators.

Paste or tape your pages up on a wall if it helps. What you are constructing is a competitive set based on every possible differentiator you can think of in the category and then listing every car brand you can think of in each place that it fits. You will be amazed at how many brands fit nowhere.

The real reason that you are doing this in such a varied and complicated category as automobiles is to discover on your own how important differentiation is, and how you can go about thinking about it. Principles are always easier to learn in a category other than your own—your thinking and judgment are then independent of your emotions and uncluttered by the facts.

As soon as you have this exercise completed as thoroughly as you think you can, we will move on to the next step.

The next step is for you to construct a similar competitive set based on the characteristics that are important and could be compelling in the category in which your brand does or will compete. In other words, do this same exercise on the category that is most relevant to you, the category in which you and your brand compete.

Here is what you are trying for: You want an expectation for your brand that is compelling enough to attract the choices of your target audience. And at the same time, you want your brand to be different enough that the necessity to choose almost goes away. You are so differentiated in such a compelling way that you become the only option in the buyer's mind.

BRAND STUDY: Was FedEx Differentiated?

In 1965, Yale University undergraduate Frederick W. Smith wrote a term paper about the passenger route systems used by most airfreight shippers, which he viewed as economically inadequate. Smith wrote of the need for shippers to have a system designed specifically for airfreight that could accommodate time-sensitive shipments such as medicines, computer parts, and electronics.

In August of 1971, following a stint in the military, Smith bought a controlling interest in Arkansas Aviation Sales, located in Little Rock, Arkansas. While operating his new firm, Smith identified the tremendous difficulty in getting packages and other airfreight delivered within one to two days. This dilemma motivated him to do the necessary research for resolving the inefficient distribution system.

Thus, the idea for **Federal Express** was born: a company that revolutionized global business practices and now defines speed and reliability.

The Federal Express expectation was differentiated "When it absolutely positively has to be there overnight."

I will bet that when he started, Fred never dreamed that business people would eventually begin to use the overnight service even when a package did not need to be there overnight.

FedEx's superior service and their superior tracking ability eventually changed the customer expectation of "speed" to the customer expectation of "absolutely reliable," and that was an expectation more compelling to an even broader market with increased usage frequency. As a result, FedEx (express services alone) now handles about 3.2 million packages and documents every business day.

Is FedEx a Killer Brand? Ask **UPS,** or ask the U.S. Postal Service (if you can wake anyone there).

Expectation Can Build a Category

Now, oddly, while your brand's expectation should compel brand choice, it can also be used to drive other things, like a category or premium pricing. For instance, in the FedEx example it was building a category (overnight shipping) and at the same time rearranging the economics of mail. Everyone complained about the cost of mailing when the stamp price went up a few pennies, but the very same people would pay the $15.00 to FedEx with no complaints in return for certain overnight delivery.

Think about the power of this brand, FedEx. Certainly the overnight promise was a huge new benefit to the category, but as people began to use FedEx for absolutely certain delivery and the ability to track a shipment, they gladly went way up in price to solve a problem that many of them had rarely if ever had. How many times in your life has the Post Office actually lost something you mailed or failed completely to deliver it?

Here is one of my favorite examples from India, an example of building a category with a brand expectation. India is a land of tea drinking. Imagine that you wanted to get people to start drinking coffee instead. Imagine the challenge of building a retail chain of coffee shops in a land of tea drinkers. That's what one company is doing.

BRAND STUDY: Coffee Day

Coffee Day is a chain of some 300 coffee shops, Café Coffee Day in India, plus some additional Coffee Day Xpress counters where you get coffee and go. I visited my first one on the highway between Bangalore and Mysore in the South of India, where it is generally humid and hot.

Unlike Starbucks or **Caribou** coffee shops, Coffee Day shops are bright and airy and look like a diner from the 1950s with red and black and chrome. And they are not all in cities and neighborhoods. Many are along the roadways, which makes sense when you think of a driver needing a pick-me-up such as caffeine offers. (No one will ever convince me that you get the same lift from a cup of tea as you do from a cup of coffee.)

Coffee Day shops are very clean-looking and differentiated from other village stops along India's roadways. They kind of sparkle, actually.

The reason that this is important is that Starbucks and Caribou are as much about the experience of drinking coffee as the product itself. And they have tended toward reproducing a warm, fuzzy feeling of coziness with their décor. Coffee Day has proven that coffee can be about the experience without being warm and cozy.

The big idea behind Coffee Day is the expectation. Every cup, no matter the location, no matter the time of day, no matter the weather, is printed with the slogan "A lot can happen over coffee." Notice that they have chosen an expectation that is not related to a product characteristic. No lift, no taste implication, no brewing connotations, just "A lot can happen over coffee."

This is one of my all-time favorite copy ideas. It is a slogan born of expectation. "A lot can happen over coffee." This expectation is relevant and rings true for businessmen, friends, lovers, thinkers. This is a slogan that rings true for us all, even for non–coffee drinkers. "A lot can happen over coffee."

They are driving the category with brand expectation. At the same time, they are riding category growth up as the leading location for drinking coffee.

Expectation Can Drive Prices

Let's examine a couple of examples of driving premium price with differentiated brand expectation. We will look at two very different brand expectations from the hotel business, one a difference in degree and the other a difference in kind.

BRAND STUDY: The Ritz-Carlton Difference

The **Ritz-Carlton Hotel** Company was founded on the principle of providing a groundbreaking level of customer service (a difference in degree). This philosophy was distilled into a set of core values called The Gold Standards: The Credo, The Motto, The Three Steps of Service, the twenty Service Values, and The Employee Promise. All 18,000 employees of The Ritz-Carlton know and embrace these guidelines, which are constantly available in the form of a pocket-sized, laminated card.

The Gold Standards are introduced at intensive orientation training for new employees, and they are are reinforced in daily departmental "line-ups" attended by all employees. The Gold Standards are the basis for all ongoing employee training, and The Ritz-Carlton is an industry leader in providing 120 hours of training per employee per year.

"Although much imitated, The Gold Standards as embodied in The Credo Card remain an industry first and are a blueprint for our success," says Horst Schulze, president and chief operating officer, on the company's Web site. "Every employee has the business plan of The Ritz-Carlton in his or her pocket, constantly reinforcing that guest satisfaction is our highest mission."

Ritz-Carlton is so serious about this guest satisfaction brand expectation that employees have the ability to meet guest expectations even at a cost. For example, a cleaning supervisor on a floor can spend up to $2,000 to solve a guest problem without asking for approval from anyone. The company trusts its employees to make good judgments and claims that it is rarely disappointed.

Next, we'll look at a hotel brand built upon a difference in kind.

BRAND STUDY: The Variety of Aman Resorts

It is generally accepted in the chain hotel business that you create a brand and differentiate it with an architectural look like **Hampton Inns,** or a location strategy like the original hotel brand, **Howard Johnson's,** or a service level expectation as in the Ritz-Carlton example.

Aman Resorts has accomplished something very different. Aman has created a differentiated and consistent hotel brand expectation despite broadly differing architectural styles, very different climates and geographies, and very different cultures and people.

Some Aman hotels are on tropical beaches, such as Amanpuri in Phuket and Amanpulo on a Philippine island. Some are in central India a hundred miles from nowhere, such as Amanbargh in Rajastan. One of their Indian resorts, Aman-i-Khás, is even a Mughal Tent village on the edge of the Ranthambore Tiger Reserve. There is Amangani in Jackson Hole, Wyoming, which looks like it might have been designed by Frank Lloyd Wright. There is an Aman in northern Cambodia surrounded by Buddhist monks.

I have been lucky enough to stay at four different Aman resorts, and they all deliver upon one common brand expectation that I can find with no other hotel brand. (And, as someone who has flown more than 3 million miles on **Delta** alone, I stay in a lot of hotels.)

Aman promises "peace." Aman delivers "peace." Everything at an Aman hotel is peaceful: the design and layout of rooms and public spaces, the privacy between rooms (the tents at Aman-i-Khás are at least fifty meters apart; the luxury huts at Amanpuri the same), the demeanor and dress of the staff, the music piped through the hotels and rooms, the incense in the air, the lack of meetings and large groups assured by having limited conference space. And this peace is very noticeable compared to other hotel experiences, however luxurious the others might be.

The advantage is that Aman Resorts are booked months in advance even with rooms starting at $1,000 or more a night. They have found a differentiating expectation that is compelling to their target audience. In fact, on your second visit, you are given a very high quality "Amanjunkie" T-shirt. And you actually become one quickly.

Aman is to other hotels as meditation is to exercise.

Let's look at one more example. Here, a brand had to create an idea to make the differentiation that it did have more compelling. No one would argue that **Grape-Nuts** are different than other cereals. No flakes, just little hard crunchy kernels that most people don't find particularly tasty.

BRAND STUDY: What Do Grape-Nuts Taste Like?

One of the first ready-to-eat cereal products ever made available to the public, Grape-Nuts was first introduced in 1897.

Made of wheat and malted barley formed into crunchy little balls like BBs, Grape-Nuts was so named because its inventor, Charles William Post, said that grape sugar was formed during the baking process and described the cereal as having a nutty flavor. Grape-Nuts also look like dried grape seeds, which they are not. In fact, Grape-Nuts have never included either grapes or nuts as one of the ingredients.

Charles Post had been a patient of the famous Dr. Kellogg at his health sanitarium. Both ended up in the cereal business because cereals were our first "health" food.

Grape-Nuts was a cereal for health addicts, and was arguably the precursor of granola.

Grape-Nuts was promoted as a natural cereal for health and vitality and was even marketed at one time as "brain food." It is probable that Grape-Nuts was even the first brand to use a coupon when Post offered a one-cent coupon to try the new cereal in the late 1890s.

In the 1950s and '60s Grape-Nuts was marketed as the cereal that "fills you up, not out."

But it wasn't until Grape-Nuts used Euell Gibbons as an advertising spokesperson in the 1970s that the differentiation of Grape-Nuts overcame the expectation of "must taste bad" and became as compelling as it was differentiating. The brand was eighty years old and came up with a great idea.

Gibbons was a naturalist and health food expert known mostly only to other health food enthusiasts. But he looked and lived the part. And he wrote a wildly successful book, *Stalking the Wild Asparagus,* in which he taught us to find food in the wilderness, even to eat parts of pine trees.

When Euell Gibbons described the taste of Grape-Nuts in the advertising, he went beyond the natural sweetness and nuttiness of Charles Post, and uttered the memorable phrase, "reminds me of wild hickory nuts." Trial of the product soared, although I have yet to find a single person who has ever tasted a wild hickory nut.

His description, his appearance, and his overall credibility just struck people's fancy. That you can make your differentiation more compelling with magic words delivered from the right source is a powerful lesson in marketing.

6

Sustain Your Differentiation as Long as Possible

In today's world, sustaining a difference is very difficult. Even if you have a patent on the difference, your protections lasts only nineteen and a half years after you first file for the patent. If it takes a couple of years for the patent to issue (and it is rarely less), you have only seventeen and a half years left.

Further, if you get a patent it is only as valuable as your ability to defend it. Often the publishing of the patent itself helps competitors figure out a way around it. And defending the patent against aggressive competition can cost more than getting the patent in the first place—much more.

Nevertheless, patents are still good and valuable. And where there is even the remote chance that you could get one, you should try . . . unless you have a trade secret that is best protected by keeping it secret. A good example of keeping something secret is the original recipe for Coca-Cola.

An NDA, a New Drug Application, is even more expensive than a patent. It takes longer to get but sometimes can be used to sustain a differentiation more powerfully than a patent, even in non-drug categories. For instance, if you make a therapeutic claim (e.g., "lowers cholesterol") for a food product and you do the clinical studies and file an NDA for the food as a therapeutic product, you can sometimes get the NDA. That means no other competitor in your category can make your claim without duplicating all of the testing and completing a filing of their own; this can take years if they don't start until after you introduce. If the claim is very compelling, you can own market leadership before they can get there to compete.

> *Your difference need not be legally protectable, but it must be tightly linked to your brand.*

Any time you make a therapeutic claim for your brand, you may need to do just as much claims-support testing as you do for an NDA anyway, so be aware that this is an option. You can file an NDA on a device or a process or service just as you can a drug or a food. It may or may not have already been done in that particular way before, but that does not mean that you can't try to. I was part of the early efforts to file and get NDAs on food products rather than drugs, and it had never been done before. You just need a provable therapeutic claim.

But let's talk about what is most likely to happen in the life of you and your brand. You have discovered or created a difference that cannot be protected. You can still sustain it if you do everything correctly and your competitors do not.

The following examples will show that you do not need a protectable difference to sustain your differentiation. You just need to make it so intrinsically linked to your brand name that it is difficult for anyone else to compete. Can that be done?

BRAND STUDY: R-R-Ruffles Have R-r-ridges

The character of "Baby Horton," and his familiar first words "R-R-Ruffles have r-r-ridges," began in the early 1950s. This was the **Ruffles** potato chips' advertising icon for more than thirty years, continuing into the late 1980s.

The ridges were added to the brand to make it more rigid than regular potato chips, in order to produce a superior product for use with dips. Ruffles are basically just corrugated potato chips. Just as a corrugation adds strength to cardboard and enough strength to a sheet of tin to make it suitable for roofing, corrugation added to a potato chip made it better for use with dips.

However, while the brand itself sustained its product differentiation with the ridges, after thirty years it walked away from its advertising. Ten years after changing the advertising, consumer feedback showed that people still remembered Baby Horton and were still imitating his pronunciation of the famous line.

Finally, Ruffles began to lose its edge, with sales declines over three years and household penetration down 25 percent. So Frito-Lay staged a rebirth, bringing back its classic Baby Horton character (after ten years in retirement) with an unusual offer. the first parents to name their baby Horton won a $50,000 college-savings account (and $15,000 to defray taxes).

Forty-nine families complied. The first got the prize. What the judges said: "It's scary that so many people remembered and named their babies Horton."

A $10 million ad and public relations campaign (not very much in today's media world) revived the old "R-R-Ruffles have r-r-ridges" tag line. Ruffles sales rose 5.9 percent to $338 million; market share rose eight percentage points.

What is reassuring is that Ruffles so completely owns ridges that numbers of competitors since the 1950s have failed to even establish so much as a private label competitor. Can you imagine owning a $300 million-plus brand with no substantive direct competitor?

The Ruffles story is a good lesson in the value of sustaining a compelling and differentiating brand expectation. The following case study provides another one.

BRAND STUDY: Slinky Continues to Walk

In 1943, Richard James invented one of the greatest toys ever. James, a naval engineer, was conducting an experiment with tension springs. During the experiment, one of the springs fell to the floor and began to "walk." James took the spring home to his wife, Betty, and asked her if she thought it was something they could pursue. Betty had an instant and, in retrospect, far-reaching vision for a toy and scoured the dictionary, looking for an appropriate name. She came across the word "slinky," a Swedish-derived word meaning stealthy, sleek, and sinuous. Toy history was made.

The **Slinky** debuted at Gimbel's Department Store in Philadelphia, Pennsylvania, in 1945. As hopeful as they were, both Betty and Richard were skeptical about how the Slinky would sell. All their doubts were put to rest when all 400 Slinkys for sale were purchased in the first ninety minutes. Since then, over 300 million Slinkys have been sold worldwide. The Slinky is still made in Hollidaysburg, Pennsylvania, with the original equipment Richard James created. The original Slinky has changed little in over sixty years (a crimp was added to the ends of the wire to ensure safe play). At $3.99, the Slinky remains a value-priced toy for children of all ages.

Though it was developed to be a toy, other applications for the Slinky have been discovered. The Slinky has been used as an antenna by soldiers in Vietnam, as a therapy tool, and for coordination development.

And most importantly, there is no other Slinky. Even after sixty years.

As difficult as it is to sustain a compelling and differentiated expectation for a brand, there are many successful examples that prove that it can be done. The following is another.

BRAND STUDY: Keeping a Brand Aloft

How many competitive brands can you think of for **Frisbee**? How simple is the product to duplicate? Seems easy, doesn't it? So why are there no successful competitors? How has Frisbee sustained itself? See if the following fun facts, taken from the company's Web site, give you a sense of how they may have done it.

* Ivy League students began experimenting with flying discs in the 1920s when they tossed around pie tins from the Frisbie Baking Company of Bridgeport, Connecticut. As the empty tins were tossed, college kids would yell "Frisbie!" to signal an oncoming flight.
* In 1948, Walter Frederick Morrison combined his fascination with invention, his interest in flight, and a a post–World War II substance called "plastic" to form a flying disc. In 1955, Morrison sold his flying disc invention to Wham-O, which introduced it in 1957 as the "Pluto Platter."
* In 1958, Wham-O modified the "Pluto Platter" and introduced the Frisbee flying disc. Printed on the bottom of each Frisbee flying disc were the words, "Play catch. Invent games. To fly, flip away backhand. Flat flip flies straight. Tilted flip curves." The product instantly became a sensation.

✳ The game of Ultimate Frisbee was invented in 1969 by high-school students in a parking lot in Maplewood, New Jersey. The first intercollegiate game of Ultimate was played in 1972 between Princeton and Rutgers. (Remarkably, Rutgers won by the same two-goal margin as it did when it beat Princeton on the same field in the first college football game 103 years earlier.)

✳ Just about everyone in the United States has heard of the Frisbee disc; nearly 90 percent of all people in this country have played with one.

Frisbee sales number in the hundreds of millions. While there are many variations for different purposes, Frisbee has stayed true to its roots and resisted the temptation to introduce Frisbee balls, board games, or tricycles. Nothing has been done to undermine the basic fundamental expectations of the brand.

Rather, Frisbee has used its compelling differentiation to turn its usage from play to sport and sustained years of interest in the brand and the category that it leads so dominantly. It is more popular today than ever.

Frisbee is a great example of sustaining your brand expectation without the benefit of solid protection.

Don't Wander Off Track

Unfortunately, the next few sections of the book will be filled with sadness. While it is difficult to find examples of brands that fit the principles necessary to sustain themselves as Killer Brands, it was all too easy to find lots of examples that have temporarily or permanently lost their way.

We all understand the nature of temptation, whether it is to eat what is not good for us or to do much worse, but apparently there is no more tempting a behavior than to expand a good brand beyond the focus that made it successful to start with. There is no other explanation for why this behavior is so rampant in the marketplace now.

Even the smartest, best companies wander off track, as you will see. Even the smartest brand managers wander off track. I have done it. Perhaps you have, too.

Let's start examining this wander phenomenon with a Source of Volume principle. There are only two ways to build a brand's volume (or sales). You either add users to your user base or you get your current users to use more. That's it.

The Source of Volume equation is this: $V = u(f)$. In this equation, V stands for volume, u stands for Users, and f stands for frequency and amount of use.

If you expand distribution and add more stores or availability and don't add users, you don't really grow. If you can't add users, and your current users don't use more, you don't grow.

Corporations have an unending appetite for growth, something that traces back to a voracious appetite for the growth of shareholder value. Every shareholder who buys stock, including owners and managers of private companies, makes her choice based on the same expectation: "This stock is going to go up."

Some might call this "greed." Not me. It's the way the world works, it's the root of human progress, and it's okay as long as you don't let it cause you to ruin an otherwise great brand.

But what a temptation it creates.

BRAND STUDY: A Tide of Progress?

When I was first married and my wife sent me to the grocery store to buy **Tide**, I knew exactly what I was supposed to buy. The only issue was which size. There was one Tide. And it always did the same thing. The brand expectation was focused and clear—even to me, and I did not do the laundry.

Was that focus and clarity enough for Tide? Well, Tide was the leader of the detergent category, and had been every single day since a few short months after it was introduced in 1945. In fact, Tide even represented a folklore story about focus that I believe to be true.

When the enzyme detergents were introduced in the early 1960s, the Tide brand-management team feared that their brand would lose its leadership because several of the new enzyme detergents were shown to outperform Tide in usage tests. The group developed a new Tide with enzymes, called Tide XK, and after much market testing and research went forward to Procter & Gamble management to gain approval to introduce Tide with Enzymes.

It is reported that the executive vice president of P&G at the time turned down the recommendation with the explanation that Tide with Enzymes was too specific for Tide, that Tide had never been more specific than merely a "washday miracle." The brand-management team argued, "We must have enzymes. We cannot compete on performance without enzymes."

The executive agreed. "Oh, you can put enzymes in Tide. You just cannot tell anyone about it."

The new, improved formula (with enzymes) was introduced as Tide XK behind the slogan "Dirt Can't Hide From Intensified Tide!" Within a year, when rumors of the skin toxicity of enzymes killed the sales of the other enzyme detergents. Tide XK (with enzymes that they never featured) gained 6 share points in a monster category.

Now, fast-forward to today. What is going on?

If my wife (yes, I am still married to the same woman) were to send me to the grocery store today with instructions to buy Tide, I would be lost. Do I buy Tide, or Cold Water Tide, or Tide with Bleach, or Tide with a Mountain Fresh Scent, or worse yet, the recently introduced Simple Pleasures detergent from Tide?

What happened to the miracle? Is including bleach a miracle? Is a mountain-fresh scent a miracle? And what do simple pleasures have to do with a washday miracle?

All of a sudden I have to think. As we discussed earlier in this book, it is not in the best interest of a brand to make a buyer think. It is not in Tide's best interest for me to stand in that detergent aisle and think.

Why? Because as long as I buy Tide with no thought, just out of habit, I am not susceptible to the lure of any other brand. As soon as I have to think, I can get confused (yes, it happens), and worse yet, I start looking around the category to see what's available. In fact, one of the best strategies for you to use to unseat an entrenched leader is to introduce doubt and cause buyers to start thinking.

In 1970, Tide represented over 50 percent of all profits for P&G despite the fact that there were over sixty brands in the company. Does Tide still represent over 50 percent of P&G profits? What do you think?

So why does a company like P&G and a brand like Tide, which used to conform to the principles of a Killer Brand, wander off like they have? Why do they violate the principles that they in part first taught the business and marketing world? My guess is that we can blame it on that inexorable need for growth. Tide may be bigger, but is it the "miracle" Killer Brand that it once was?

Since we have seen this wandering with both Crest and Tide, does that mean that some form of wandering is inevitable? No, I don't think so. We have other case studies in previous pages that show that wandering is not an inevitable consequence of growth and dominance. What can we learn from other examples?

There are very few brand successes that can rival the resurgence of **Harley-Davidson.** Harley-Davidson owners are not just loyal. They love the brand. They love the icons that surround the brand. There are very few brands that have ever stretched their loyal user base from Hell's Angels to CEOs.

What is the compelling differentiation for Harley-Davidson? Research shows that it is the "Harley lifestyle." Some owners live it. Others just lease the lifestyle for the weekend. But it is the expectation of that lifestyle that drives the brand and continue its success.

In what ways does the Harley lifestyle allow them to expand the brand? The brand values are strong, masculine, and rugged. Sure seems like there is lots of room there.

Why then did executives introduce a Harley-Davidson perfume? But they did. They also tried Harley-Davidson wine coolers. I know that this is difficult to believe, but it's true.

The Harley crowd was not impressed. It is lucky for the brand that these efforts failed miserably before they had a chance to do much damage.

Don't Overextend Your Brand

I think every brand has a pivot foot, as in the sport of basketball. As long as you keep that specific foot planted, you can move one step in any direction. But you cannot change to a different pivot foot. In basketball you must dribble to move your pivot foot. There is no such thing as a dribble in brand management.

Your brand's pivot foot can be its compelling differentiation, like Crest. It can be even more specific and be form-related. If your compelling differentiation is "fizzy relief," as in **Alka-Seltzer**, you may be able to expand from antacids to fizzy relief of cold and flu. But the minute you also start offering gel tabs, as Alka-Seltzer did, you are walking in terms of basketball. You are wandering.

In the world of brands, if wandering does not work, it does not hurt your brand very much. But if it does work and sticks in the marketplace, you have taken a major step toward dissolving the very focus that made your brand successful in the first place.

Don't be guilty of wishful thinking. Just because users in some form of research give your brand permission to overextend, don't do it. I have seen research that gives Levi's permission from consumers to make motorcycles. I have seen research that gives **Rawlings** permission to make hot dogs. I have seen research that gives **Raleigh** the permission to make auto-mobiles. This kind of research is hog-wash. If you clearly understand what your pivot foot is and why it is what it is, you will instinctively know what you cannot expand to without stretching the limits of your brand.

> Know just how far you can extend your brand without diluting it.

If you want a real education in huge mistakes made by brands, many due to wandering, I recommend you read Matt Haig's book *Brand Failures* (Kogan Page, 2003). You will discover that **Smith & Wesson** tried to make mountain bikes, that **Bic** made under-wear, that **Pond's** introduced toothpaste, that **Colgate** tried to market kitchen entrees, and many more examples that are equally astounding.

Okay, so you cannot overexpand your brand. You are not allowed to wander. What can you do when your brand approaches the limit of appeal from the focus that you have chosen?

Go back to the Source of Volume formula. You can only grow by adding users or increasing usage by current users.

So, first, when your brand approaches maturity, you can add new ways to use it and to realize the same or slightly different expecta-tion. Second, when your brand approaches maturity, you can use the existing expectation to add users by making the expectation more important.

There are three illustrative examples in the following case stud-ies: **Arm & Hammer Baking Soda, Johnson's Baby Shampoo,** and **St. Joseph's Aspirin.** The Arm & Hammer example shows how you build your brand by giving users another way to realize their expectations. The shampoo example shows ways to increase the number of users by slightly repositioning the expectation that consumers already have. The St. Joseph's example shows how to add users by finding a completely new use based on the expectation that it always had.

BRAND STUDY: Another Box of Arm & Hammer

For almost 100 years of its brand history, Arm & Hammer Baking Soda was used primarily for cooking. Individual users developed folklore around the product concerning its abilities to absorb odors. They noticed this magic ability because if they left the open box of baking soda too near something smelly (like onions), the baking soda took on the smell.

Marketing did nothing about this for a long time because the baking business continued to grow and a rising tide floats all ships. But then the American home began to change. With the advent of convenience foods in the 1950s, American women no longer cooked as much. Baking soda sales growth was nonexistent and threatening to reverse.

Of course the management at Arm & Hammer knew of the odor-absorbing qualities of baking soda, so they began to promote the brand to use for more than just cooking. Then an outside creative source came up with a brilliant idea.

Put an extra box of baking soda in your refrigerator to keep it smelling fresh. It works so well, in fact, that today there are more homes with a box of Arm & Hammer in their fridge than in their pantry.

What's more, the expanded usage idea for Arm & Hammer led consumers to find more and more ways to use baking soda to deodorize. Then the company subtly let them know that it was also a great nonabrasive cleaner for stainless steel pots and pans and sinks and other items.

Today you can buy Arm & Hammer baking soda in a shaker can for cleaning, in a box designed to increase air flow while in your refrigerator, in a large box for pouring down your toilet to increase enzyme growth in your septic system, in forms to use to deodorize your carpets and cat litter boxes, and more.

What used to be a $50 million brand of baking soda is now a company of almost $800 million in sales in just baking soda variations. How's that for expanding your focus without losing it?

Right down a Princeton, New Jersey, road from Church & Dwight, the company that owns Arm & Hammer, is the consumer division of Johnson & Johnson. They have a very good story also.

BRAND STUDY: It's Gentle Enough to Use Every Day

Johnson & Johnson owned the baby shampoo category with No More Tears Shampoo. Not only was this shampoo gentle on a baby's fragile hair and skin, it also did not sting the eyes, and so over time virtually every mother used it.

Once the birth rate in America leveled out and started to decline, so did the sales of J&J Baby Shampoo.

Luckily, just as women were slowing down their frequency of having babies, they were also going to work, with more and more of them getting jobs every day. It was not enough to wash their hair once a week, or have it done at a salon. Working every day meant showering in the morning. More and more, tub bathing shifted to showering.

Looking fresh every morning at least five days a week and taking showers instead of tub baths meant a rapid increase in the frequency of shampooing. The shampoos on the market for adult women were too harsh and cleaned too effectively for use every day without damage to the hair. Only one shampoo would do. And it was a baby shampoo.

J&J recognized that and starting advertising J&J Baby Shampoo for women who had to wash their hair every day: "Gentle enough to use every day." This idea made plenty of sense and fit into the brand's existing expectation that it was mild because it was made for babies.

Soon J&J Baby Shampoo was a leading brand of shampoo among women, with sales for women almost forty times larger than the baby market on any given day. Did this on-strategy method of repositioning the existing focus to add users and frequency of use work to build a mature brand? You bet it did.

The baby shampoo phenomenon hit around 1970. In 1980 when I was president of Neutrogena, we introduced Neutrogena Shampoo. It was what is called a "bland" shampoo, meaning we used very gentle ingredients, although more expensive ingredients than were in baby shampoo.

We did it to be consistent with the Neutrogena image of purity and safety to sensitive skin. Research showed that we had a built-in user base just by making "Neutrogena for your hair." The research was right. Then a miracle happened. We developed and introduced the compelling and differentiated expectation covered in the example on page 34, and Neutrogena Shampoo's volume grew eventually by 4600 percent.

The following is one more example of parlaying an existing brand expectation into a much larger brand idea. It comes from the world of babies again.

BRAND STUDY: Once a Day Reduces Heart Attacks

Doctors have long known that an aspirin a day reduces the chance of a heart attack because of aspirin's ability to thin out blood, the same ability that reduces the pounding in your head.

However, aspirin also makes your stomach bleed—or at least does so among enough people to prove problematic for daily use.

Bayer and other aspirin suppliers conducted clinical studies on the amount of aspirin necessary to deliver the cardiac benefit. At the same time, aspirin was being tied to Reye's Syndrome in babies and killing sales of all baby aspirins.

Enter St. Joseph's children's aspirin, which was essentially just a smaller dosage than adult aspirin. You guessed it. St. Joseph's was already 80 mg, the dosage recommended for cardiac health, and of course it already had the reputation of being gentle enough for babies, so it was repositioned for adults.

Today millions of adult Americans take St. Joseph's baby aspirin every day for their heart, many more than the number of headaches and toothaches possible among babies, even if every one of them had one or the other every day.

This completes the section on Focus. You have learned that Focus itself is to be valued. You have learned that your Focus should be compelling. You have learned that your Focus should also be "differentiated," and you have looked at several methods of differentiating. You have learned that Focus can be sustained without wandering. And you have learned how to increase the power of your Focus without wandering.

If you now value Focus itself regardless of what focus you choose; if you have chosen a focus that is compelling enough to manage the choices of the individuals along your Chain of Choice; if your Focus itself is differentiating or you have found a way to differentiate it without detracting from its compelling nature—you are ready to proceed to the second step, **Alignment.**

Focus itself is powerful. Alignment multiplies that power exponentially.

THE SECOND STEP: KILLER ALIGNMENT

7

Align Everything You Do

This section of chapters is about multiplying the power of your focus without changing the focus. The secret to multiplication of power is in coordination.

There is a measure of animal efficiency in the world of zoology that determines how many calories of energy it takes for a given animal to move one pound of its own body one foot. Technically this is called *positive work efficiency* (PWE). It is derived from *mechanical power output* (foot pounds) divided by *metabolic power input* (calories).

Simply put, an animal's PWE is a measure of efficiency, which in turn is a function of coordination.

Animals vary in efficiency based on the ratio of total body weight to the weight of skeletal structure. The higher the body weight in relationship to skeletal structure, the less efficient an animal is and the more calories it must consume to move one pound of itself one foot.

The lower the body weight in relationship to skeletal structure, the more efficient an animal is and the fewer calories it needs to consume to move one pound of itself one foot.

Further, this efficiency is increased if the animal's skeletal structure is arranged around an articulated backbone. In zoological terms, vertebrates are more efficient than nonvertebrates.

As examples, snakes have a high percentage of their body weight in skeletal structure arranged around an articulated backbone and a lot of skeletal mass in relationship to body mass. Snakes are very efficient. That's why some species of snakes can eat so rarely and still thrive.

Earthworms, on the other hand, have no skeletal structure, much less a backbone, thus they are very inefficient and must eat constantly to move. They have no structure to offer resistance to force, just muscular contractions. Imagine that you were just a blob with no skeleton and you decided to move across the room. Think of the effort. This is similar to the task facing an earthworm all the time. They must consume calories just to keep moving. The trail of excrement they leave behind is testimony to their voracious appetite per pound.

Brands seem to work the same way. The more coordinated the strategic structure that a brand is arranged around, the more efficient it seems to be.

In physiology, muscular strength is also a function of coordination. The more fibers in an individual muscle that contract together and the more fibers in the opposite muscle that, at the same time, relax together, the greater the strength of the muscle at that given moment.

That's why well-coordinated skinny people can be stronger than poorly coordinated muscular people. More of the correct fibers in a given muscle work properly at the same time. When you see a truly clumsy person, you can tell that their muscles are just not working together as the Creator intended.

Are you getting a clear picture here of the value of coordination? When the right hand does not know what the left hand is doing, it detracts from strength and from efficiency.

Your brand will behave exactly the same way, as will your team, your division, and your company. Coordination is the key to maximizing the effectiveness of any chosen Focus.

The Power of Alignment

The purpose of **Alignment** is to create coordination, which in turn multiplies the power of your focus, both adding strength to your focus and adding efficiency to everything that you do.

In Alignment you want to make sure that everything you do contributes to delivering your focus and making that focus obvious to your prospects and users—and, just as importantly, does absolutely nothing to detract from your focus.

Alignment is relatively easy to think about. It is very difficult to do. I firmly recommend that you create a written Alignment document for your brand and use it regularly to help make decisions. We call this document a Brand Backbone Strategy, and from the example of physiological efficiency, you can certainly see why.

By the way, when you start developing complete alignment—figuring it all out and writing it all down—you will have elevated yourself into, from my experience, the top 2 or 3 percent of all brand marketers. This is hard work, and most people and companies just don't have the intellectual vigor and discipline to do it.

So here is an area where you can set yourself apart fast. Give your brand a strategic backbone.

I have hundreds of brand backbone documents, but in fairness to their rightful owners, I cannot publish any of them in this book. On the other hand, this idea of a written alignment document is much better understood when you see the description for each strategy section integrated with an example of a real one.

So I have invented for this book a fictional brand and created a fictional brand backbone for it. Hopefully this will make the principle of alignment more clear, and give it the power in your mind that it so deserves.

Create Your Brand Backbone with Strategies That Feed Each Other

Your Brand Backbone Strategy is *a long-range statement of goals and the strategy to reach them.*

Do not confuse strategy with tactics. A strategy is a long-term plan that sets a course of action for the foreseeable future. It sets a specific objective or goal for its function and spells out the broad means for achieving the goal. Tactics are execution—how you go about it for this year, this campaign, this sales drive.

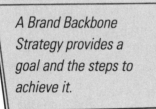

A Brand Backbone Strategy provides a goal and the steps to achieve it.

Remember, the first and most important characteristic of strategy is "long-term." In a perfect world, strategy would never change. The world of marketing is dynamic, competitive, and far from perfect. You saw in the examples at the end of the last chapter that the world does change. That doesn't mean that you should revert to tactics. It means you should set strategy for the foreseeable future. Nor does it mean that you should never change. Crystal balls are seldom completely clear, and significant unanticipated marketing developments could upset the best strategy the day after it is written. It is time then to develop a new strategy, not to resort just to tactics.

Nonetheless, if your Brand Backbone Strategy is well-conceived, well-written, and well-constructed and your foresight even average, it will take a significant event to make you change your strategy.

The following is an outline of commonly used sections in a Brand Backbone Strategy. Based on the specifics of your product or service, you may not need some of these sections, and you might need to add some more. Think carefully about the kinds of decisions you will have to make for your brand in the future, and create a strategy to guide every one of those decisions.

In these sections, you'll see a description of each part of a typical Brand Backbone Strategy and then, following each description, the relevant part of the fictional backbone developed for the fictional brand Tickets for Two.

Situational Review

A concise one-paragraph statement of the current situation and the key factors that are relevant to your brand opportunity or brand challenge serves as helpful background to the brand backbone itself.

Airfares continue to grow more and more expensive at the same time that airlines struggle more and more with making the profits necessary to survive. Fewer than 16 percent of flights on any given day are sold out. Average capacity utilization is only 68 percent. Airlines become significantly more profitable as capacity utilization grows beyond 68 percent. *[REMEMBER, I am making these numbers up for this book. This is a fictional example in a nonfiction book.]*

At the same time, over 40 million Americans are retired or semiretired, giving them great travel flexibility. They'd travel more if the costs were lower. It makes sense for airlines to add passengers above 68 percent capacity even at half revenue realization, but there is no current method for doing this.

Differentiating Concept

It is so much easier to realize your business objectives when you have a brand based on genuine and compelling differentiation, as we discussed in the previous section of this book. Emphasize its importance to the entire brand strategy by stating it simply here.

What is the fundamental thing that makes or will make your brand different from other brand choices?

> Tickets for Two will be a new method for purchasing airline travel. You will reserve two tickets (two for the price of one), but you will only be able to fly on planes that are undersold.
>
> Tickets for Two is different from standby because you will be notified by e-mail twenty-four hours in advance when capacity to your destination is available, and you have first-come first-served priority on those seats, which you can confirm online via return e-mail.
>
> If, for any reason, you do not accept a seat on the first plane offered, you will be continually notified of availability until you have used your reservation.

Long-Range Business Objective

Here, you set a long-term objective for your brand. Don't use a specific number that could become obsolete next year or in five years; rather, set a goal such as achieving (or maintaining) market leadership in sales or market share, or an annual growth rate. Some products start out with limited life spans, to serve a limited purpose. If so, state that here.

Your objective can be stated as long-term growth, accelerated growth, category leadership, an expanding margin of leadership. Just make it long-term and single-minded.

Your strategic objective must be *clear, measurable* (state how, here), and *achievable.*

> Tickets for Two will seek to become a leading source of revenue for struggling airlines, and intends to become a major brand within the total sphere of air travel.
>
> The specific long-term objective is to build at least a $3 billion brand with a gross profit margin of no less than 7 percent. This objective requires that we sell 20 percent of currently unsold airline seats, generating 10 percent of their revenues for them because of the two-for-one pricing. Where these numbers are achieved, virtually any of our partner airlines will become profitable. *[REMEMBER, this is fiction.]*

Need

State the specific market need that your product or business fills. Dimensionalize the need. How serious is it? How unfilled is it? How long do you expect this need to exist? Is it recurring, or does your product fill it forever?

> The primary target audience needs access to lower-priced travel to enrich their lives. Many of them worked for years and years to enjoy retirement and are finding that, with rapidly rising costs, their dreams are more expensive than they had projected. They need enriching life experiences because they no longer have work to fill that role in their lives. Every day tends to be the same, so they also have a need for variety. Market research shows a strong target need for a sense of adventure and excitement in their days.
>
> The partner target (airlines) has a need for higher revenues without associated higher costs. The best way to create higher revenue with roughly the same costs is through better capacity utilization.
>
> It is to both of these needs that this brand will be addressed.

Target Audience

To whom are you marketing? The more precise you can be here, the better. Avoid broad common denominators and easy target statements. Tell everything you know about your target: who they are, what they buy and use, how they make their choices, where they get their information, etc. Your brand marketing target should always be narrower than you expect your user base to be.

> The total target audience for this brand includes anyone to whom the promise of two-for-one tickets is attractive, but the primary target audience, the audience against which all messaging and spending will be focused, is retired couples less than eighty years old. The key here is to target spending

toward "time to travel," "desire to travel," "spontaneity," and "flexibility of planning." Thus the brand's primary target is not best described demographically, but attitudinally and behaviorally.

A primary target couple could be fifty years old, having been lucky enough to retire early, though seventy years old and up is more typical of the majority of the target. An age of eighty has been arbitrarily set without the data to support it based on the anecdotal sense that people begin to age out of travel mode at about eighty. Note that this cutoff is for spending purposes. We may very well do significant business among people over eighty, but market research suggests that as you age, if you continue to travel, you will likely choose group tours, and plan farther ahead, and not be the spontaneous target for this brand.

A secondary target will be unmarried twosomes—man and woman, man and man, and woman and woman. Unmarried twosomes are secondary because without the coordinated schedules that exist with married couples, they are likely to have slightly less spontaneity. If the unmarried twosome happens to share living quarters, coordinated schedules are more likely and we will treat them as if they were married for targeting purposes.

The partnering target is to sign up as many airlines as we can get, concentrating on desirable destinations that do not often get discounted.

Source of Volume

What will be the primary source of volume for the brand? Will it be adding new users, or having current users buy more of the product(s)? This decision will be very important in the communications of the brand.

Use the equation $V = u(f)$, where volume always equals the number of users times the frequency and amount of use.

You have seen some very creative uses of this equation.

Source of volume will likely come from episodic usage, a broad base of users taking advantage of the brand less than once per year. We hope to develop these episodic users into regular users, using the brand at least once a year. The brand is further likely to develop heavy users who use three or more times a year, but we expect heavy users to be less than 10 percent of our total user base.

Of course, until introduced and marketed for awhile we will not know this for sure, but all of the brand's initial financials will be based on 90 percent once-a-year average usage, and 10 percent three-times-per-year average usage.

Core Expectation

Restate the singular core expectation for your product. It should be compelling, sustainable, and differentiating. Everything about your business will be aligned to this single core expectation. It may or may not be stated verbally and/or explicitly to your target, but if you do your job correctly, it will become the meaning of your brand in the target's mind.

The core expectation for this brand will be "small victory," as in a small winning lottery ticket, not a jackpot.

It is important to note the emotional benefit inherent in this core expectation of "small victory." This brand will be about a lot more than just saving the money. It's about choosing a destination together, prepaying at less than half-price, and being pleasantly surprised when your opportunity to fly comes up. You know you are going to win, just not when.

The Old Course at St. Andrews works like this. You cannot reserve a tee time. You can only enter a lottery for a tee time. You find out in the morning whether you came up or not. You know you will win if you stay around long enough, but you don't know when.

Brand communications will feature the excitement experienced at the moment of the "win."

Brand Promise

What one thing does your brand promise as a benefit to your user? Consumers are promise-loyal, not brand-loyal . . . and your brand must stand for a promise in your potential user's mind. This promise should naturally flow from, and be supported by, the core expectation. The promise is what is said or implied to set up the expectation.

> Unlike a true lottery, the brand will promise the target audience a guaranteed win; you just don't know when.
> The promise will be delivered always in a way that appeals to the target's sense of adventure. The promise will be delivered as something like "Sure, you get half off the tickets, but it's way more exciting than that."

Basic Business Strategy

State here the relationship of your business to the owners of the business. Examples can be building the business to sell, using the business as a strategic advantage that helps another brand, using the brand to generate cash to fund R&D or expansion, etc. Answer the questions as to why this brand business should exist.

> This particular business is being started to hold longer term. It will serve to generate income and employment for the entrepreneur as well as build net worth for the owners. At the time of its founding, no future liquidity event is yet envisioned.

Basic Marketing Strategy

State here the most fundamental framework of your basic marketing or business thrust. Limit yourself to three lines. If you cannot state your basic marketing strategy in three lines, you don't have one.

> The basic marketing strategy is to partner with airlines for inventory, and market prepaid tickets directly to the target audience.

Behavioral Objective

What one thing do you want your user to do that, if they did it, would allow you to reach your business objectives? Be specific.

> The behavioral objective for consumers is to become regular users, no matter their frequency. Our objective is for our users to consider us first any time they decide to travel as a couple, even to visit relatives or children. We want to be their option of first choice.
>
> The behavioral objective for partner airlines is to sign up with us, regularly deliver us timely inventory (forty-eight hours in advance), compete for best opportunistic pricing with other airlines going to the same destinations, and help us promote the brand.

Hopefully you are beginning to sense the power inherent in perfect Alignment—in getting this all sorted out and written down, so it can be approved and understood by all parties relevant to the business of your brand.

8

Brand Fundamentals and Brand Mechanics

All of the strategies in the previous chapter can be considered the foundation of the brand backbone. In this chapter, continuing with the fictional example of Tickets for Two, we will explore the function of the substrategies, which will differ slightly for different kinds of brand businesses.

Brand Fundamentals

These substrategies define what your brand will be, and what your brand will do.

Positioning Strategy

This is a statement of how you intend for your product to be perceived by the target. State it in the form of the three-part positioning: *usage positioning, personal positioning, and product positioning.*

In other words, state how and when your brand is to be used, in what way the user will be different because he chooses to use your brand, and in what way your product or service is different from other choices available to the target user.

> The usage positioning for this brand that we wish to occupy within the target audience's mind will be "This is always the brand to use when you want to travel with another person and are flexible as to timing."
> The product positioning for this brand within the target audience's mind will be "This brand is easier to use than shopping the myriad of airline prices and schedules. Just tell us where you want to go and we'll name the special price, and keep delivering options to you until you take one."
> The personal positioning for the brand within the target's mind will be "This is the brand of travel that vibrant, still-with-it travelers choose to use."

Product Strategy

What are the fundamental strategic elements of the product? How often must it be improved? In what directions? For a new product, these are invention guidelines. For an existing product, this is guidance for Research & Development. Also include information about the breadth of the brand, if applicable: should it be available in different sizes, colors, strengths, etc.? What are the strategic purposes of the different sizes, colors, strengths, etc.?

> The focus of the product strategy will always be "two for." No single tickets will be sold. No group tickets will be sold.
> The product strategy will focus on desirable destinations where discount air fares are rare (for instance, Las Vegas would be off strategy because of the constant low-cost flights available) and will build the range of destination options available as rapidly as possible.

The strategy is to offer tickets only with airlines that can give the company remnant inventory forty-eight hours ahead of time so we have time to forward that inventory choice to ticket holders via e-mail. And we want only airlines that allow us our normal commission (7 percent) on the sale and require us to forward payment to them only after a flight option is chosen and booked.

In the foreseeable future, the brand will offer only airline, train, or cruise tickets for two. No accommodations will yet be included, but will be considered in the future after the brand is well-established.

The brand may expand into tickets for two for local events such as plays, shows, and sporting events, but that is a down-the-road decision.

Packaging Strategy

This section should cover functional configuration, delivery system, and graphics. It should deal in strategic terminology (for instance, if the target is teenage girls, the bottle should be strategically sized and shaped to fit into a teenage female hand). This seems very simple, but write it all down as completely as you can. You will be surprised at the strategic inconsistencies that can occur here.

The packaging strategy also focuses on the "two for" aspect of the brand. Further, the packaging strategy will be entirely virtual and electronic with no hard paper receipts, tickets, etc.

Naming Strategy

State not the name, but what the name should connote. What are the strategic elements? Even for an existing brand, a statement of this strategy can be helpful in deciding how and how not to use the name, as well as how to name product variations, improvements, etc.

> The name for the brand should connote fun and excitement for two people. Exotic would be okay, but not mandatory. Since usage will be infrequent and the product itself is virtual rather than physical, the brand name should also be very distinct and memorable. Tickets-for-Two should be the descriptor, not the brand name.
>
> Both the brand name and the Tickets-for-Two descriptor should be protected by trademark if possible, using travel services as the category generic.

By the way, since this brand backbone is being developed for a fictional business, I am going to choose a brand name right here and now that is consistent with this naming strategy. The name will be TANGO Tickets-for-Two. After all, "It does take two to TANGO."

Logo Strategy

Usually the logo communicates as much as the name does about the brand. What will the logo connote? How and when will it be used? Are the logo and the name always used in concert, or are they ever use separately—and if so, how and when?

> The logo should be designed to improve the memorability of the TANGO name. Remember that this logo will be the only physical manifestation of the brand appearing in newspaper ads, on Internet banners, in AARP mailings, etc. So it is very important for the logo to be memorable itself and contribute to the verbal memory of the word "tango."

Copy Strategy

I recommend five short paragraphs here. First, reprise what behavior you want the target to practice. (This is to remind yourself constantly to make your communications and actions behavioral.) State the benefit promised to the target consumer in return for the intended behavior. Then state the support for believing the promise is true. Then state the emotional dimension to the promise. Lastly, decide the tone of the advertising and the personality or character you wish the brand to have.

> We want target consumers to make TANGO Tickets-for-Two their travel service of choice when they are traveling in a twosome.
>
> When a target consumer goes to *www.tango42.biz,* she will benefit from the easiest way to plan and book discount tickets to desirable destinations. She just checks a destination from an alphabetical list, and we give her the prepaid price compared to normal fares for two.
>
> The incredible TANGO prices are available because they are not tied to a specific date, but rather based upon unsold seats, and first-come first-served response to an available date.
>
> Advertising will add excitement to this new chance to get a great trip for two for less.
>
> Advertising will build for the brand and its users a character of "adventure."

Pricing Strategy

Are you pricing on costs, competition, or to produce an image? Are you to be priced at market, above the market, or below the market? Why? Once stated, how do you decide when to change? Don't list dollars. List the principle.

> Our pricing strategy is to base our price for a two-person package to a given destination as low as we possibly can, taking into account our need to maintain at least a 7 percent gross margin between what we sell for and the cost we negotiate from the airlines for remnant inventory.
>
> In addition to our 7 percent gross margin, we will also make a profit off of earnings on the float between when a consumer prepays for a destination and when he eventually chooses an offered time slot. Depending on destinations

105

and the flow of timing options, the average ticket float could be as much as several months. For budgeting purposes, we have assumed an average float of fifteen days.

There is room in the packaging and pricing strategy for dual destinations, either/or packages, multiple destinations/ pick one, etc. to keep the idea fresh and to underscore and add to the excitement of the brand.

An important part of the pricing strategy is to allow any customer to cancel their deal and get their money back at any time if they change their mind or are unhappy with the time slots they are offered.

As long as they get a good flow of time availabilities, research suggests that outright cancellations will be less than one per cent (0.7 percent). We will charge a $25 cancellation fee, and, since we have virtually no cost involved in the original transaction, we will actually make money even on cancellations.

Note that the pricing strategy in this fictional brand backbone is more thorough than the other strategies because this is essentially a buy-and-resell business model. This pricing, costs, spread, and float are all very strategic to success.

Distribution Strategy

Where is the best place for your target consumer to find your product? What part does distribution play in how your product is perceived? And how will you physically get it there?

The TANGO product itself will be distributed online through a Web site and by phone. Availabilities after purchase will be communicated to the customer's e-mail and also by computer phone notification if they select both options.

This product may also be distributed through select catalogs (e.g., Travel Smith) and other direct-response mediums.

Partnering Strategy

Many products require a partnership to execute correctly—a retail partner, a manufacturing partner, a sales partner, etc. Each of these requires a strategy, detailing factors that would be important in a partner and the strategic parameters of a beneficial partnership. Later, you will be able to hold up potential partnerships against this strategy and easily identify those that meet your product's needs.

The TANGO partnering strategy is with as many airlines as meet our two principle requirements for partnership.

The first is communication of remnant inventory at least forty-eight hours in advance of flight. The second requirement is pricing low enough to allow us a minimum 7 percent gross profit from the price at which we presold the trip.

Brand Mechanics

The following substrategies define how the brand will use its resources and go to market. It also includes the financial strategies needed to achieve your goals.

Advertising and Media Strategy

The media strategy states how you will reach the target with the message—once again, in broad strategic terms, not in plans for the year. How important is reach? How important is frequency? How important is timing?

TANGO will advertise directly to consumers. We will concentrate on effective frequency against the target audience rather than reach. We will focus on seasonal timing toward the end of each season when people are most ready for a change. We will focus on non-summer months when families and children are not traveling.

We will advertise in every medium that will allow us to buy last-minute remnant time from them, or pay on a per-order basis. This includes TV, radio, newspaper, Web, etc. All advertising will be direct response, "do-it-now" advertising featuring toll-free numbers and Web sites. Where possible we will take advantage of discount pricing often offered for direct-response advertising.

Sales Promotion Strategy

(*Note:* A promotion is a special offer for a temporary amount of time. It is not a permanent offer from the brand. Even continuity promotions like airline mileage can be ended without changing the brand.)

Consumer promotions: If you promote, what are you after? Trial, repurchase, loading, increased usage? Which sizes are best promoted? How frequently? Will you promote everywhere? Or regionally? Will you schedule for seasonality or holidays?

Trade promotions: What can you reasonably expect the trade to do to help you reach your objectives, and how will you promote to achieve that?

> This entire brand has a promotional feel to it, so promotions will not be used on an ongoing basis.
>
> We will use promotion to build our initial user base as we enter each new city. We may do special promotions with affinity groups filled with our target audience, e.g., the AARP.
>
> We will use promotion to announce new destinations now available through TANGO. We will not promote to the trade (the airline industry).

Merchandising Strategy

This strategy deals with what you wish to see at retail level. What section and where on the shelf? How set, visualized, augmented?

> The brand itself is virtual. However, we will use the same retail "take-with" cards that the credit cards use. This will be a form of merchandising. Take-with cards will be in ticket offices,

retirement homes and neighborhoods, senior centers, restaurants in target cities and neighborhoods, organizations
filled with our target audience, etc.

Publicity Strategy

This deals with the non-paid media. Will publicity for your product help? Is it possible? What kind do you want? How important is
it? How will you achieve it?

> TANGO will use free publicity efforts proactively, attempting
> to get introductory coverage when we enter a new city, and
> then later "true trip" feature stories in all of the same media
> that we choose as advertising mediums.
>
> In certain media like *Modern Maturity* or the Costco news-
> letter, we will work to see if we can establish regular articles
> in every issue under themed trip ideas or something similar.
>
> We will also seek free publicity online. When possible we
> will offer free trips through TANGO as prizes on game shows
> and "makeover" shows, etc.

Internet Strategy

The Internet is a factor for almost all businesses, whether you
choose to participate in it or not. Consumers learn about your
products and your competitors' products, compare prices, and even
purchase over the Internet. What role(s) will the Internet play in
your business: e.g., customer service tool, distribution channel,
marketing tool?

> The TANGO Internet strategy is two-fold:
>
> First, we will use the Internet and phone (supported inter-
> nally by the Internet) to deliver our product options to the
> customer, then to inform them when their "ship comes in."
>
> Second, we will advertise on all Internet sites related to a
> given destination that we offer, including the Google search
> pages when that destination is searched.

Extension Strategy

Will there be line extensions for this brand, or not? What would the strategic implications be of line extensions, and to what types of products would the brand be extended?

> Other modes of travel (e.g., train, bus, limo, cruise) will be considered valid line extensions of the brand, as well as accommodations and package trips like Club Med. However, no extension of the brand will be introduced in any market until at least Year 3 of TANGO availability in that market.

Management Strategy

What human resources will be allocated to achieve this brand's objectives? How will they be guided? Controlled? Motivated? Evaluated? Compensated?

> This business will begin with management by the owner/founder, assisted by a minimum staff of project-hired freelancers.
>
> All employees will be incentivized to be helpful, enthusiastic, and polite to the customer, with a can-do attitude and a commitment to help resolve issues and fulfill dreams. An ongoing mystery shopper program will be used to find examples of off-strategy customer service and weed them out. Drawings at least monthly of on-strategy employees will be held, with the prizes TANGO Tickets-for-Two.

Manufacturing Strategy

Where will the product be produced? One location? Local plants? In-house? Subcontracted? What are the strategic reasons for this manufacturing plan?

> The service will be manufactured and delivered entirely electronically via Web-based software.

Sales Strategy

How will you see that your distribution strategy is executed? What else do you expect from field sales on behalf of this product?

A sales force will be used to develop airline partners and maintain the relationship.

A direct customer sales force will be tested for TANGO. This sales force will give presentations and promote the service at gatherings of the target audience, such as garden clubs, senior events, churches, etc.

External Resource Strategy

What kinds of external resources will be utilized and for what strategic reasons?

Since the company will be managed with as few full-time employees as possible, external resources will be used strategically for the following: mystery shopping and customer feedback, market research, advertising development, and media planning and buying.

Spending Strategy

How will you decide in any given fiscal period how much to spend on marketing? How will funds be split between advertising, promotion, etc.?

Introductory marketing will be based on task budgeting. For example, what amount of spending is required to build awareness within a given target? We will spend when necessary against target pockets until we can afford to build broader awareness in a community served.

Ongoing advertising will be budgeted at no less than 40 percent of the 7 percent gross profit spread. This 40 percent spending rate will continue unless the brand begins to oversell the inventory available by such a large degree that we can fulfill customer expectations. Remember that every new customer prepays and establishes a credit on which we make a profit on the float. If we begin to get customers far in excess of inventory, we will cut spending in that area, and consider turning down orders.

Investment Strategy

Are you willing to investment-spend in this brand? Or is it a cash generator? On this business, how long are you willing to place your investment at risk?

The strategy is to investment-spend by location for no more than twelve months. If we are not breaking even on a month-by-month basis in a given city by the end of twelve months, we will consider exiting that city.

The company is raising the capital necessary to lose money for the first thirty-six months of operation.

Risk-Aversion Strategy

How will you strategically develop a plan to limit risk, or facilitate recovery?

TANGO will be introduced city by city and target by target to limit risk. We will make sure that we are tracking toward success before we add geography.

There will be no national advertising, no Rose Bowl or Super Bowl advertising, only super-targeted direct-response efforts.

Testing Strategy

For this brand, what kind of testing policies are strategically sound? Marketing research, ad research, simulated or real test markets, promotion tests, other strategies?

The most important thing to test and track on the TANGO brand will be hits and calls based on different messages and mediums. There will be an ongoing effort to learn about individual activities and their conversion rates, as practiced by other direct-response mediums such as catalogs.

Expansion Strategy

This strategy deals with the geographic expansion of the brand. When do you expand? When do you not expand? For what strategic reasons?

We will add cities for advertising and access to additional consumers only when we are tracking to success in cities already served. Keep in mind that in each city we enter, we must also develop relationships that create ticket inventory that leaves from that specific city.

When we are successfully serving at least forty of the top metro areas in the United States, we will consider testing expansion into foreign markets. We will choose foreign expansion markets based on the concentration of qualified target couples.

As you can see from the preceding principles of alignment and the fictional example of TANGO Tickets for Two, there is a lot to think about in bringing a brand into perfect alignment.

But I will testify to the following based on twenty-five years of structuring brand backbones for clients and for our own ventures. You yourself can add this alignment exercise to virtually anything that you are currently working on; your brand effectiveness will increase by a minimum of 20 percent and your brand efficiency will increase by a minimum of 10 percent.

These gains will be realized using the same focus that you currently have. (If in fact you have a fuzzy focus, trying to construct a brand backbone around it will make that fact self-evident rather quickly.)

And these gains from alignment will come into play even before we get to the third principle of the Killer Brand, **Linkage**.

It is not easy to construct a good brand backbone, but it costs you nothing except time and intellectual sweat to at least try. Feel free to send questions concerning clarity on this principle to me at *flane@franklaneltd.com*.

In the next chapter, we are going to look first at brands that appear to be in alignment, and then at brands that are not in alignment because of some obvious and easy-to-see activity. Keep in mind that these are examples I've chosen with no inside information as to what any of these brands are attempting to accomplish. I am just looking at them as you would, from the outside.

9

Execute on Strategy Without Exception

It is virtually impossible for a team of intelligent people to actually go through a brand backbone exercise, structure one for their business as thoroughly as the example we went through in the last two chapters, and still have major parts of the backbone end up out of alignment.

More likely, the exercise of bringing everything into alignment will prove so rigorous intellectually and emotionally for the team that the effort will be abandoned or postponed and never finished rather than completed in an insufficient way.

Do yourselves a very big favor. Please ask for outside help before you and/or your team abandon this exercise of alignment. You will thank me for this suggestion. I know this for sure: the power of having everything and everyone pulling in the same direction at the same time is absolutely exhilarating. There are no other words for it.

Now, as I've said, I'm not privy to whether such a written document exists for the following brand examples, but reviewing the way they execute in the marketplace suggests strongly that they understand and practice alignment however they get there.

The first two, both clothing companies, are both relatively new brands, so one could argue that they have not had the time yet to wander or get out of alignment. Nevertheless, they are well worth looking at.

BRAND STUDY: Just Relax, Tommy Bahama

I believe that **Tommy Bahama** is a brand born of the Jimmy Buffett "parrothead" fan base, which seems to endure and expand as new generations of fans age into it.

Like Jimmy Buffett himself, Tommy Bahama is a lifestyle brand. A laid-back lifestyle is the philosophy of Tommy Bahama.

Tommy Bahama has in a few short years successfully created a perfectly aligned clothing brand, then expanded that brand expectation of "relaxing" to restaurants, home furnishings, and more.

The brand's ultimate goal is the weekend that never ends.

Established in August 1992, with corporate headquarters in New York and Seattle, Tommy Bahama is a lifestyle company that defines elegant but relaxed tropical living with men's and women's sportswear, denim, swimwear, accessories, and a complete home-furnishings collection.

Examine the way that this brand has crafted its various lines to be in perfect alignment with the basic brand philosophy of a laid-back lifestyle and the brand expectation of an endless weekend. The following are some examples of their brand language, taken from their Web site:

"Tommy Bahama: Purveyor of island lifestyles. Relaxed fashions for men and women. Island-inspired accessories. Store and café getaways. Private oasis home collection.

Men's

No man is an island . . . but who wouldn't prefer living on one? Experience an elegant and relaxed array of island-inspired clothing fashioned in our signature prints, and crafted from the finest cotton, denim, linen and washable silk.

Women's

Fashion infused with the spirit of all things tropical, and crafted from luxurious and sensual fabrics. For a woman whose sense of taste and refinement is inspired by what she loves, whether it's clothing, a breathtaking sunset, or the boundless ocean.

Accessories

Ignite adventure and fun with our eclectic collection of accessories. After all, the secret to never-ending weekends is in the tropical details.

Island-inspired getaways

Take an island getaway to a Tommy Bahama store. It's a treasure chest of home decor and exquisite men's and women's fashions.

Visit a Tommy Bahama Tropical Café: a sumptuous and inspired menu awaits, with delectable entrees, snacks and cocktails.

Private oasis home collection

Live the island every day; there's nothing like the rejuvenating spirit of the tropics throughout your home."

America once had another brand that was similar to Tommy Bahama and perfectly aligned around a somewhat similar idea. It was called Banana Republic. The original Banana Republic clothing was all based on safari design and the original stores were reminiscent of small remote countries. The stores and the clothing instilled imagination and the urge to explore. It was a perfect brand.

Then overnight it jumped into hot water, sold out, and went mainstream into bland clothing and me-too store designs with no differentiation at all. After watching the de-branding of Banana Republic supposedly led by changes in clothing fashions, it will be interesting to watch the next ten years of Tommy Bahama.

Now let us examine another aligned brand example, one that prefers to be spelled without capital letters.

BRAND STUDY: Clothing as a Healthy Lifestyle

The **lululemon athletica** company was founded in 1998 by a group of visionary athletes, in response to the dramatic increase of female participation in sports and the belief that yoga is the way to maintain athletic excellence into an advanced age. As their Web site says:

"lululemon athletica is a yoga inspired athletic apparel company. We aim to provide components for people to live longer, healthier and more fun lives. Founded in Kitsilano, Vancouver—one of the healthiest places in the world—the first lululemon store not only featured a design studio / retail store but also shared space with a then fledgling yoga studio.

Authentic to its West Coast roots, lululemon continues to focus on a healthy, balanced fun-filled way of life.

Life is filled with runs at the beach, hiking, biking and a walk to work, a yoga class or a 15–30 minute coffee with your best mate."

The target audience is clearly women—moreover, women with a certain yoga-related lifestyle that includes exercise activity, meditation, and good eating habits. Lululemon athletica manufactures, distributes, and retails clothing to these women via its own stores and wholesales out to other retail stores in North America and internationally.

Lululemon design is created from the feedback of athletes and customers. The original lululemon store was a design room surrounded by a retail store. Today, the lululemon design and production teams use interactive feedback from lululemon customers to adjust the fit of their products, detect new athletic trends, and discuss desired fabrics.

Lululemon recognizes that women have been embracing outdoor sports and exercise in unprecedented numbers since the 1990s. The company sees a direct correlation between education and athletics and a stronger immune system, and understands the need for versatile, functional, and better-fitting feminine technical clothing.

The company offers complimentary yoga classes to staff at local studios, allowing educators (the company's moniker for retail salespeople) to experience and understand yoga, health, and movement therapies. This enables them to connect with the brand's communities and communicate their understanding of both the lululemon lifestyle and lululemon clothing to their customers.

Lululemon is a good example of brand alignment.

I hope it is clear from the lululemon example how motivating alignment can become for your own employees as well as for your target audience. I love the fact that they call their in-store employees "educators."

Now let's look at two variations of the same brand, one undeniably aligned and the other which has been in and out of alignment.

BRAND STUDY: Disney World Versus the World of Disney

If you have ever visited either **Disneyland** or **Disney World** you have experienced one of the great examples of the principle of Alignment existing anywhere.

What is the core expectation? Let's call it family fun—not kid's fun, not teenager fun, not adult fun, but family fun. Is Disneyland aligned perfectly to produce family fun? Or better yet, is there anything that exists at Disneyland that is inconsistent with family fun?

Is the layout aligned? Are the rides and attractions aligned? Is the pricing aligned? Is the décor aligned? How about the activities? The food? The employees?

Is the sense and feel of Disneyland more aligned and consistent than Knott's Berry Farm right down the road, or Six Flags in other locations, or Coney Island in Cincinnati? I think so.

A good example of alignment is the Human Resources policy at Disneyland and Disney World. They don't call employee recruiting just "recruiting." They call it "casting." That's because they have developed aligned specs for every single job that exists at Disney, and they cast specifically to fill those specs. They don't just have employees. Disneyland is run by characters in a family-oriented day of entertainment and clean, wholesome fun, a stage show in which you and your family participate.

Disneyland and Disney World are true Killer Brands. In fact, Disney World has literally created an entire metropolitan area in central Florida and put Orlando on the map as an emerging city. This proves the power of Killer Branding.

Disneyland and Disney World are of course owned by a major public corporation by the name of the Walt Disney Company, which owns many other brands.

As the parent company is broadly known and referred to as **Disney,** is it, too, aligned? The answer is different depending on when in history you ask it. If you asked about the alignment of the parent company up until about the 1970s, the answer would have been yes. If you had asked in the late '80s and '90s, the answer may not have been such a clear yes. But it is apparent that the corporation understands alignment much more clearly now.

For instance, all of the Disney neighborhoods, vacation living resorts and destinations, Big Red Boat cruise ship, etc. are firmly aligned to the Disney brand expectation of family fun. Their entire Parks and Resorts division is very well aligned.

Their consumer products divisions are well aligned. Disney movies are once again Disney movies.

When the corporation acquired Miramax films, it spun off the off-strategy Dimension film unit, including *Scream* and *Scary Movie*, to the founders of Miramax, who did not stay with the company.

ABC is called the ABC Family Network in Disney's corporate literature, but let's face it, not everything on ABC is family fun. **ESPN** is also owned by Disney as part of ABC, and many of the talk shows on ESPN are clearly not for family consumption. But from an alignment standpoint, this is okay because neither ABC nor ESPN is included or managed under the Disney brand, just as neither Tide nor **Dawn** is managed under the same brand expectation, yet are both owned by Procter & Gamble.

However, if the Walt Disney Company owned and produced entertainment under any brand name that was clearly detrimental to the Disney image that has produced a $32-billion-a-year empire, it would be a brand alignment no-no, and that used to be the case a few years back when Disney made a few movies and other business decisions that were clearly off-strategy. Now that Disney is back on track, it shows that they understand which properties belong with which brand.

Congratulations to Disney for returning to Killer Alignment to sustain what clearly is a Killer Brand.

The following case study is about a brand with many similarities to the lululemon brand, except that they have an issue with alignment. I am not sure how they are going to handle it over time. Let's take a peek at the pack business.

BRAND STUDY: Give Me a Tough Backpack with Daisies on It

JanSport built its reputation in the serious backpacking and mountaineering categories. The brand expectation was reliable performance in the wilderness. This required new materials, great engineering, and rigid quality control, all of which JanSport developed and delivered backpack after backpack.

The brand was developed by mountain climbers who knew what was needed and what was not yet available. As a result, they created and built the leading brand for serious use. They became the market leader in backpacks and gear for this serious segment. And as outdoor activity continued to grow, they rode the wave to higher and higher sales. Jan-Sport was clearly a Killer Brand.

Then young people started taking backpacks to school. This trend developed in college, then spread to high schools, then to elementary schools. And of course, some of the young people who knew JanSport from their outdoor activities starting wearing JanSport packs to school.

It did not take long for the school market to grow to be a lot bigger than the wilderness market, and JanSport grew with it.

But as the school market grew, it developed based more on fashion and aesthetic design than on performance characteristics. This strategic fish of another color swam by JanSport and the brand bit.

Now JanSport does well over half of its revenue in the school market, and well over half of those units are designed to look good and to be differentiated by surface designs—colors, patterns, licensed designs, etc.

Can a backpack with an overall daisy design be a performance backpack, even for gardeners? You tell me. I have worked at all ends of the cereal business—the nutrition end, the taste end, and the licensed characters for children end. And you will never convince most moms that **Flintstones** cereal is as nutritious as **Wheaties**. I think there is a similarity here. Not only do performance and fashion rarely fit together under the same brand, but they don't even behave the same.

Performance endures and you know where and how to work to improve upon it. Fashion comes in and goes out. This year's Flintstones are next year's Dinosaurs.

Engineers develop and improve upon performance. Artists and designers create fashion.

There are executives at JanSport who admit they have a strategic inconsistency, but no one has successfully addressed it and solved it yet. Is JanSport still a Killer Brand? Business-wise, the answer is still yes. Principle-wise, the answer is no.

Business results have a way of catching up to principle.

Keep an Eye on Your Alignment

A brand out of alignment is like the proverbial frog in hot water. If you throw a frog in hot water, it will immediately jump out. However if you put a frog in cold water and turn on the heat, the frog will sit there as the water gets hotter and hotter until he is cooked and never notice the degradation in his living conditions until it is too late.

A brand out of alignment is often the same way. No one throws your brand in hot water. But the water that you put yourself in can get hotter and hotter if you do the wrong things. Your brand will get fuzzier and fuzzier until it is out of focus and in trouble. It might take a few months. It might take a few years.

Important: The longer the brand degradation takes, the harder it is to see, the more damage is eventually done, and the more difficult it is to fix.

There is only one solution for the marketer. You must be constantly vigilant that your efforts to grow your brand do not also "no" your brand.

One of the classic problems in alignment is pricing. It is fairly obvious to most of us that if your core expectation has anything to do with saving money, you have to be careful to be aligned with your pricing strategy. But how many of us are as clear on the other end of pricing?

> *People expect to pay more for a brand they consider to be better.*

Examine alignment with me. Do you really believe that a brand that claims to be superior in degree when it comes to performance is going to be less expensive than the brands that it claims to outperform? Do most people believe in "something for nothing"? I think not.

If your Brand B is better than my Brand C, then it makes perfect sense for your brand to be priced a little higher than mine. It makes okay sense for you to be priced the same. It makes no sense for you to be priced lower.

First of all, your lower pricing is out of alignment with your promise of superiority. People expect to pay more for better. Second, you are leaving money on the table that you could be spending in marketing to build awareness, availability, or persuasion. A great brand marketer never sells at any price a penny lower than necessary to execute the brand's strategy.

Distribution can be an alignment trap. Can a cosmetic sold only at **Wal-Mart** ever be as good as a cosmetic sold only at **Saks**? What if you reverse the story? Can a cosmetic sold only at **Neiman Marcus** be worse than a cosmetic sold only at **Walgreens**? People infer certain value and performance expectations based on where they find your product.

Can a product sold only at convenience stores do a good job of reaching career women, who research shows do not like to go into convenience stores?

Packaging can be an alignment trap. Can a cosmetic with cheesy packaging command as high a price as a cosmetic with elegant packaging?

Targeting can be an alignment trap. Can a movie that appeals mostly to teenagers be sold to empty-nesters? Can a two-passenger car be sold to a mother with four children? Can a van be sold to a bachelor with no need to carry anything?

Don't Shoot Yourself in the Foot

The preceding examples of misalignment are obvious ones. But alignment problems hide in the smallest places, too.

We once worked on a dry-eye product. It was targeted at older people who wear eye glasses. The usage instructions were critical for performance and safety. Not a single person in the target audience could read the usage instructions because the type was too small. Is this an alignment problem?

Alignment can also offer positive opportunities to differentiate in a compelling way. We also worked on a medication for treating glaucoma, an eye condition that threatens to proceed toward blindness if treatments are not followed religiously. The problem is that people with glaucoma tend to be older and often cannot remember whether they have taken their medicine at the right time. We helped develop an aligned form of packaging, a bottle that when you close the cap snaps to the next time you are supposed to take it. This compliance cap, "c" cap for short, helped save some indeterminate number of users' eyesight. Not a bad benefit for humanity just from thinking through alignment, is it?

> Names need to be in alignment with the expectations people have for a brand.

Do you honestly know when you put the box of Arm & Hammer Baking Soda in your fridge? Do you know when to replace it? The principle of Alignment helped the company develop a new form of package, recently introduced, that counts off time once opened and tells you when to replace it.

I just took a break from writing and noticed my wife's dressing table. There are cosmetic products there for use around her eyes. By definition she cannot use them without removing her glasses. But without her glasses, she cannot see how to use the product—not just the instructions, but how to hold the product to use it.

Naming can be an alignment trap. **Value Jet** may communicate low prices, but does it communicate safety and competency? Start with the assumption that people will expect the worst and confirm their expectations when the worst happens. It is interesting to me that all major airlines have a crash every now and then, and don't go out of business. But the very first crash that Value Jet had put it out of business. It is a much more sound brand now that it has been resurrected and is named **AirTran**.

You may think that these issues of misalignment are not as important as I am making them in this chapter, but seriously: would you hire a brain surgeon to remove the tumor from the head of your five-year-old child if his name were Elmer Fudd?

Even typography can be an alignment trap. Would you hire a law firm if their name were spelled out in handwriting script? Would you buy a new computer if the logo for the brand were in Gothic type? Would you buy a new SUV brand if the font style for the logo looked like a dress ad from the '50s?

Robert L. Shook wrote a book called *Winning Images* (Macmillan, 1977) in which his thesis was that there are certain principles that drive winning images; these are defined as any image others choose to follow. Thus his book looked at the principles inherent in diverse leaders: on the one hand, Hitler, whom millions followed and believed in, and on the other hand, Jesus, whose image eventually won over a major portion of the earth.

Two of the principles that Shook isolated in his book were the principles of stability and dependability. He used the example of how important it can be for an insurance company or a bank to have their name on the top of a high-rise building. It makes them appear to be stable whether they are or not. This is also a principle of Alignment. Is it important for the bank to appear stable? If so, how does that affect the strategies underlying packaging, location, and building choice?

Shook further used the example of a friend who is dependable versus a friend who is somewhat scatterbrained and not dependable.

What do we as humans always gravitate to? Do we prefer to be around instability? Do we prefer to be around irresponsible, unreliable people?

Well, the same is true for brands. Do we prefer to be around irresponsible, unreliable brands? This is in part what Alignment is about.

When I went to Neutrogena, believe it or not, there was no budget for product formula testing. Here was a company that used its name on every single thing that it sold. One big product failure on hand cream or a issue with a potentially carcinogenic ingredient in soap could negatively affect the image of every other product in the line, yet there was no routine testing of ingredients or formulas other than those required by law.

The company had no idea when it put a new soap item on the market whether its intended users would like it or not. As long as the chairman who owned over half the public shares liked the product, it was released to market. And in Neutrogena's case, the chairman was not even a target user.

If you looked at what should have been the brand backbone for a company using the same name on everything, then safety testing and user performance reactions would be a very important part of the strategy and a necessary ingredient in every go-forward decision.

We of course fixed that issue, but this is part of what Alignment is about. What sections of your total brand business strategy are always critical? How can you ensure dependability and reliability?

The first step is getting all of your necessary and critical alignment strategies written down. The next step is executing consistently with the written strategy. And the only way to do it is to be vigorous in your vigilance.

The point is: when aligning your strategies as in the brand backbone example for TANGO Tickets-for-Two, you must think through every possible issue and brand behavior strategically before you are faced with making brand decisions. Then all you have to do when the time comes is to execute on strategy.

I heard a football coach being interviewed after halftime of a game in which his team made as many first-half mistakes as one can make. He said, "Whoa, what's that down there at the end of my leg? I believe it's my foot. I think I will shoot it!" He went on, "Now guys, how much sense does shooting yourself in the foot make? If you are bound and determined to shoot a foot, please shoot the other team's foot."

Well said, methinks.

Every single section of a brand backbone, or of a thorough alignment document of your choosing, represents the opportunity to align all the elements of your brand and bring strength to it, or to misalign and weaken your brand.

Remember, real Killer Brands do not have self-induced weaknesses.

Adopt One Simple Operating Technique

This section will teach you one technique that will mean more to the long-term health of your brand than you can imagine.

First, get your team together. If you don't have a long-range alignment document such as a brand backbone for your brand, create one together. Make sure it has a section for every kind of decision that your team will ever need to make. You cannot have too many sections.

Make sure that each section is about strategy, not tactics. Go back in this book and reread the section on the outline of a brand backbone, skipping the sections of the TANGO example if that makes it more clear. If you have a retail store, realize that you need to add a location strategy, a real estate strategy (buy or lease and why), etc. Once again, if you have a question about what should be added to a backbone for your type of business, e-mail me.

Work on this document together until everyone who is important to the daily operations of the brand is in agreement and every strategy is in alignment. If you work for someone else, get their input and then their approval. I personally like to have brand alignment documents approved in writing, by all brand constituents.

Once you have an approved brand backbone alignment document, make sure that every person on the team has his or her own copy and understands the meaning and logic behind each strategy. Be sure to include outside resources such as designers, ad agencies, media firms, PR agencies, sales agents, etc. Get everyone on the same page. Let everyone know that you do not expect to entertain ideas or recommendations that are inconsistent with the approved strategy document.

Now, here is the magic part.

Don't have a meeting or a discussion on your brand without a copy of the brand backbone present at the meeting. When considering an idea for action, or a decision, or a recommendation, ask the following three questions in order:

1. Is this recommendation consistent with the backbone strategy?
2. If not, can it be modified to bring it into alignment with the backbone strategy? If the answer is "no" to both questions 1 and 2, abandon the recommendation and give it no consideration. No matter what, don't do it.
3. If the answer to either of these questions is yes, ask yourselves, can we afford to do it now?

The yeses to this question matrix represent your pool of on-strategy action options. Don't do anything that is not on strategy. Get as much done as possible of those things that are on strategy.

Don't agonize over whether an on-strategy recommendation may or may not work. If it requires a really big investment, test it. If not, just get it done.

I will personally warrant that if you get a lot of things done and executed in the marketplace, and they are all in alignment and consistent with your brand backbone, enough of them will work that you will begin to give your brand the elements of "killer" status. It always works out that way.

In baseball it is said that you cannot walk your way to the majors. The same thing is true in brand marketing. You cannot take pitches and never swing. You will never hit a home run if you don't swing. However, if every swing is on strategy—e.g., aimed at a good pitch—you will hit a few and you will eventually hit homers.

The number of hits determines your marketplace success. On-strategy actions that do not work do not cost you much. As long as you stay on strategy, batting average is not as important as you might think.

On the other hand, when you approve something that is off strategy, you are just swinging at a bad pitch. You will strike out a lot. No hits means no action in the marketplace.

And remember this: If you do something off strategy and it happens to work, you just shot yourself in the foot. In the Brand

Studies earlier in this book, you have seen example after example of off-strategy actions. And you have seen examples of on-strategy actions.

Since I criticized Tide for wandering, let me give on-strategy credit and kudos to another Procter & Gamble brand for a new development that I just saw on TV this morning.

An On-Strategy Extension

Dawn is a dishwashing liquid that is differentiated in its ability to cut grease. Today I saw Dawn in a new form factor described as "Direct Action Foam." It was pretty cool. It came out of the bottle directly into your pan or on to your sponge as foam and when used on a pot or pan, the grease just got eaten up. Grease just disappeared.

In fact, Dawn's Direct Action Foam is so effective at cutting grease that you don't even have to use water. Most of us would not neglect the rinse, but it sure cuts down on water consumption, an added compelling expectation that is on strategy as long as reduced water consumption is proof of Dawn's ability to cut grease faster.

Stay on strategy like Dawn does in this example. There are always lots of new things that you can do and/or add that are actually on strategy. Give your brand meaningful chances to move forward and run the bases. Don't shoot yourself in the foot. There are plenty of other brands in the marketplace who will be shooting at yours. Don't do it to yourself.

Even in cowboy movies, killers don't last long when they keep shooting their own selves in the foot.

THE THIRD STEP: KILLER LINKAGE

10

Execute Killer Linkage

We are now done with most of the hard work. Finding the best focus is sometimes difficult. Staying on focus is always difficult. Creating and maintaining alignment takes a megadose of discipline. All of this is very hard work.

I won't go so far as to say that creating linkage is not hard work, but it is definitely fun. Linkage is the glamour part of the business, whether it's in concept, name, packaging, or advertising.

And great linkage pays dividends for a long time.

Pay particular attention to this assertion. It will do you little good to get the best focus in the world, and align your brand perfectly to that focus, if your target audience does not remember your brand and does not tie your focus to your brand. That's where linkage comes in.

I have no idea how old you, the reader, are at this moment. So you may or may not be able to answer this fill-in-the-blank question. But I'll bet that many of you will know the answer.

Here is the question: "You'll wonder where the yellow went when you brush your teeth with _____."

What brand of toothpaste said this? When did they start saying it? And when did they stop saying it?

BRAND STUDY: Where Did the Yellow Go?

If you answered, "You'll wonder where the yellow went when you brush your teeth with **Pepsodent**," you were right. Pepsodent starting using this advertising to differentiate themselves in the early 1950s. The brand was already popular enough to be the subject of a big Times Square sign in the original 1933 *King Kong* movie. The sign was there in the recent remake also.

But Pepsodent introduced a whole new expectation to the oral care category back when the majority of the population smoked cigarettes and suffered from yellowing of teeth.

Pepsodent is still around. It just isn't a major brand anymore, much less a Killer Brand. It is currently distributed mostly through discount stores and America's many "dollar stores." Instead of offering a powerful and compelling brand expectation, it is now marketed as a value brand.

The brand management team at Church & Dwight, the company that now owns Pepsodent, doesn't know exactly when Pepsodent stopped using this advertising, but we're all pretty sure that this advertising hasn't run in over thirty years.

The fact that so many people still remember this brand and this slogan will show the power of great linkage. I'll bet in a quantitative study on an even, fair basis right now that Pepsodent, which was the first brand ever to own tooth-whitening as a core expectation, would score quite well as a whitening brand, particularly among the over-fifty audience.

Isn't it interesting that a full generation and a half after a brand stops using communications featuring really great linkage, it still gets credit for its core expectation? Sure the original technology, Irium, is old hat now, but Pepsodent's core expectation is more compelling than ever.

I believe that any brand name that has been so powerfully linked with a core expectation can be resurrected in a major way if the core expectation is still compelling and relevant and the brand restages it by using competitive or superior technology. Thus Pepsodent could make a comeback. The core expectation of whitening has suddenly emerged as one of the most compelling expectations in oral care. Tooth-whitening last year was a $500 million subcategory inside of oral care. And there are a multitude of new whitening technologies, and at least one totally new one I know about on the way.

Slap new whitening technology into Pepsodent, and reintroduce the brand. Such is the enduring strength of great linkage.

A Memorable Slogan Is a Battle Cry

Pepsodent rhymes with "went." Rhyming is one of a number of mnemonic devices that help you remember something. You don't have to rhyme. But you do need to be memorable, not just for cutting through the clutter, but for making the brand expectation memorable. "Please don't squeeze the Charmin" is not exactly a rhyme, but the continuing dramatizations of the irresistible squeezability of Charmin made the brand expectation of irresistible softness memorable.

Sometimes linkage can be visual. The packaging for **Yellow Tail** wine is a good example of visual linkage. There is no way you can look at the packaging and not think of the brand name, and you can spot it from thirty feet away. The advertising for **Absolut Vodka** is a good example of visual linkage. The layout of every ad mirrors that shape of the bottle. The Rock of Gibraltar along with the line, "Own a Piece of the Rock" is memorable for **Prudential** and its brand expectation of stability.

In the world of advertising and marketing that I live in, there is no such thing as a tag line. I don't use them myself. Instead, you should find your brand a real slogan or a visual mnemonic device.

> You want to have a real slogan, not a mere tag line.

"You'll wonder where the yellow went when you brush your teeth with Pepsodent" is a slogan. "Please don't squeeze the Charmin" is a slogan. What makes these statements slogans instead of tag lines? Each line is a slogan because each summarizes the core expectation of the brand "in a memorable way." Most tag lines don't even fit the commercials that they are attached to.

The core expectation of your brand will never be enough. In the real world, core expectations are generally too dull to make people sit up and take notice. You must make your core expectation exciting. There is a huge difference between powerful advertising and a concept board on film. You must make your brand's core expectation memorable and tied to your brand name in the memories of your prospects.

When a brand has a real slogan, you craft the advertising message around the slogan. We learned that in Alignment. "It takes two to TANGO," is a slogan. It helps you remember the brand name and what you can expect. You can craft any number of brand campaigns around this line itself, and every one of them will be consistent with the brand backbone strategy.

That's because the word "slogan" comes from the Gaelic word *sluagh-ghairm*, which means the battle cry or war cry of the clan. I learned that from *Macy's, Gimbel's and Me* (Simon & Schuster, 1967) by Bernice FitzGibbon, the copywriter responsible for both

the "Nobody but nobody undersells **Gimbel's**" slogan as \
"It's smart to be thrifty" for **Macy's.**

In my book (and that's where we are right now), the Gimbel's slogan produces better linkage than Macy's. First, it uses words in a more interesting way—"nobody but nobody." Second, it includes the brand name.

Where have we heard an interesting use of words similar to the Gimbel's slogan that makes a core expectation more exciting and more memorable? How about "When it absolutely, positively has to be there overnight"?

Accept that there is nothing namby-pamby about a real slogan. A real slogan is the battle cry for your brand. "Tag line" means added on. "Slogan" means you are willing to fight for it.

Make Sure Your Brand Gets the Credit It's Due

When I first discovered that there was such a thing as marketing and advertising as a career—which did not occur to me until I was a junior in college and switched from a joint math and physics major to journalism—I thought linkage, or in the language of that time "brand name recognition," was everything. I believed that high unaided awareness was all a brand needed to succeed.

I tended to gravitate to "cute" linkage. Some of my favorite campaigns were for Dave's Ski Shop—"Our business is going down hill"—and The Pants Shop—"Every season is our slack season."

In advertising class, I wrote such classics as (over a photo of Jane Fonda wrapped up in beach blanket with her **Honda**) "I'm kind of Fonda my Honda," and, in an attempt to sell party-givers on serving coffee rather than alcohol, "Host 'em and toast 'em with **Postum**." These were all classwork.

I finally figured out after two years in the real world that there was more to brand success than cute advertising, and switched from copywriter to brand management trainee at Procter & Gamble. But I never actually lost my commitment to brand awareness, brand name registration, or what I now call in this book Linkage.

139

I was delighted in my training at P&G to find out that Norm Levy and Gibby Carey in the old Copy Department (P&G referred to advertising as copy) had analyzed hundreds of P&G commercials and determined that commercials that featured the brand name in the first ten seconds produced significantly greater marketplace success than commercials that didn't. Our agencies fought this tooth and nail. They fought against what they thought were rules.

I believe that there is a difference between a rule and a principle. Rules are often established arbitrarily—"because I said so." Principles, on the other hand, are derived from experience and many, many cause-and-effect analyses. If an analysis of 400 advertising commercials shows that putting your brand name up front makes your advertising four times more effective than leaving it for the end, and you are spending $10 million to run that advertising, why in the world would a smart person not follow the principle?

Let me offer a reason I now think that this specific principle works. I know from PowerPoint presentations to clients that a reference point helps make additional slides more clear and memorable. For instance, if we are talking about Customer Learning, every slide that pertains to that subject has a titled back reference, a heading or label that relates to customer learning. It helps keep the audience from getting lost.

I think advertising may work the same way. In television, if the brand name is not clear up front it is too easy for you to get lost in the story. As things unfold, there is no way to relate them to the brand in your memory if you don't know what brand the advertising is for. For instance, I see a small boy riding a bicycle down a street but I don't know what brand the advertising is for. Is it bicycles? Is it clothing? Is it a brand of small boys like the Boys Club or the YMCA? The footage is interesting because of the scenes he rides through and the people he meets along the ride. The announcer track is running on phantom video. In other words, the copy has nothing to do with the boy riding down the street. At the very end of the spot we realize we have been watching a spot about protecting your children with accident insurance. Let's call it Wilson's Insurance. There is nothing memorable or linkable here.

Now imagine you are watching the same footage, except that up front over the first scene the announcer says that some accidents would be more devastating than others. We see the boy riding through the village. At least we know this is about accidents. And we know that we don't want this kid to have one. At the very end we are introduced to Rider's Insurance, accident insurance for kids, bikes, skateboards, ATVs, snowboards, skis, etc. I think that this would be a definite improvement. You can make up your own mind.

> *Your advertising copy needs to be seen in the right context to be effective.*

Now imagine yet another commercial. Same footage, except that the announcer says up front, Rider's Insurance for Kids. He goes on to talk about risks, and unknown hazards. A car scoots in front of the boy and he barely stops in time to keep from getting hit. Every scene in the commercial is now processed in our minds within the context of the brand, Rider's Insurance for Kids.

Context is the key idea here. If your advertising copy is seen and heard within the context of your brand linkage, there is an exponentially greater chance of it being remembered accurately. This is just my theory, but it makes a lot of sense, doesn't it?

How many times have you tried to explain an ad that you saw and perhaps even liked and said, "I don't remember what it was for?" When you say this, recognize how different you are from your typical audience. You are either in the business of brands and advertising or interested enough in the business to have read this book so far. Think about how little attention someone not in the business would be paying. If you cannot remember what the ad was for, how can they remember what the ad was for?

Let's try an experiment together. Close your eyes and think back about ten years. Try to remember a commercial that ran at least ten years ago. Try to pick a commercial that you remember well, but don't remember what brand it was for. It could be television, radio, whatever. Just remember it well enough to describe it for me, but it has to be for a brand that you don't remember.

You can't do it, can you?

Isn't that interesting? We can remember a piece of drama that we experienced in a commercial last night even though we cannot remember what brand it is for, yet we can't remember the same unlinked message years down the road, perhaps not even a few months down the road.

On the other hand, if I ask you what brand asked, "Where's the beef?" I'll bet that you can remember it was **Wendy's.**

If I ask you what brand dramatized an upset stomach with "I can't believe I ate the whole thing," I'll bet that you can remember Alka-Seltzer.

That's because even though the brand name is not in the slogan used for the advertising, at least the slogan dramatizes and links to the core expectation of the brand. "Where's the beef?" tells you that Wendy's makes bigger hamburgers than the competition. Bigger hamburgers are relevant to your life whether you like them or don't like them. So your mind remembers.

"I can't believe I ate the whole thing" is relevant to almost everyone's experience. At some time we have all eaten more of something than we should have, and we have felt awful because of it, particularly when we tried to go to sleep. Do you think it is a coincidence that the man in his discomfort sits on the side of the bed, while his wife is peacefully sleeping, and groans, "I can't believe I ate the whole thing?"

Now, since you could not name and tell me about an old commercial in the absence of remembering the brand it was for, try instead to remember the oldest advertising you can remember for any brand. See if there was not significant linkage between the brand expectation and the brand's name in the ads that you remember from your childhood.

The following case study describes one of my oldest ad memories.

BRAND STUDY: The Height of a Piggy's Ambition

This one goes back a long way. I am not even sure where the brand is now. But I still remember the song in the commercials. It went:

"The height of a piggy's ambition, from the day he is born, is to grow big and good enough to be a **Frosty Morn,** so everybody join in . . . . and sing it over and over and over again, Frosty Morn."

Frosty Morn was a brand of ham from my childhood. What chance that I would remember any of these words if the height of a piggy's ambition had not been linked to growing up to be a Frosty Morn?

By the way, after I wrote this, I did a Google search for Frosty Morn ham and apparently some small company in Alabama still owns it, but I have neither seen nor heard this advertising in perhaps fifty years.

Effective Ads Always Create Linkage

Don't let yourself be fooled about this principle of linkage. If you have not already encountered the following situation in your career, you probably will encounter it eventually. It is very sad.

Big-time creative directors of big-time agencies sometimes are more interested in building their books than they are in selling your brand. That's because they impress other agency people with the books, and they get hired for a better job because of what other agency creative people think of their work, not because they happened to sell a lot of your product. In fact, creative directors that I know have admitted to me that they have never once been asked about how well their advertising worked to sell their assigned brands when they were being interviewed for a new job. Scary, isn't it, since they use up most of your marketing money?

143

As a result, they will often try to talk you into commercial executions that don't say anything about your brand. They will try to talk you into commercial executions where the viewer watches the whole spot before they know what brand the advertising is for. They will try to talk you into pretty, stunning executions that do not set up your brand's core expectation, much less burn in your brand name and link it to that expectation.

As a result today's television is flooded with advertising with weak or no linkage to the sponsoring brand. Trust me. This advertising cannot work as well as it could if the brand name came through strong and clear and was memorably tied to the core expectation from frame one.

CLARITY OF DESIGNER WORK SUFFERS

In 2006, the *Financial Times* ran an article entitled "There's more to a brand than its catwalk." The article is subtitled "As designers vie for maximum exposure at the shows, the clarity of their work suffers."

The article pointed out that designers turned to even flashier presentations at that year's Fashion Week in Milan, and that to get attention there they introduced designs that were inconsistent with their own brand images. This sounds a lot like advertising that is more memorable itself than it makes the product.

The show should never outshine the brand.

But not all big-time creative directors are about building their book. Some of them will want your brand to succeed as much as you want it to. (In this section of the book, I will use a lot of examples directly from my personal experience. I don't necessarily want to, but these are cases that I know very well, and cases where I can safely share a lot of detail without violating anyone else's confidentiality.)

The following is an excellent, and in fact overwhelming, example of burning in a brand name created for one of our ventures by Drew Fagan, who used to be an executive creative director at McCann Erickson.

BRAND STUDY: Ring Mr. Ching

Mr. Ching was a gourmet Chinese delivery restaurant chain that we developed and introduced into Atlanta, Georgia—really great food, but only for delivery. We chose the name Mr. Ching to rhyme with "ring"—a rhyming requirement that was contained right in the naming strategy in the Brand Backbone Strategy for Mr. Ching.

We only had a few restaurants to start with, and we felt we could build awareness and make people call and order (behavioral objective) better with message frequency than with reach. And frequency during afternoon drive time was the key to reaching prospects when they were trying to decide what to have for dinner. So our principal advertising medium was drive-time radio.

Drew Fagan, a truly great advertising man, created the following sixty-second introductory radio spot.

"[Tap, tap, tap sound effect.] Now class, we are going to learn the conjugation of the verb Ching. I ching. You ching. He, she, or it chings. We ching. You ching. Theeey [all drawn out] ching.

Now to make the word "ching" refer to delicious Chinese food, change it to Mr. Ching. I Mr. Ching. You Mr. Ching. He, she, or it Mr. Chings. We Mr. Ching. You Mr. Ching. Theeey Mr. Ching.

Now to have this delicious Mr. Ching Chinese food delivered right to your doorstep, just Ring Mr. Ching. I Ring Mr. Ching. You Ring Mr. Ching. He, she, or it Rings Mr. Ching. We Ring Mr. Ching. You Ring Mr. Ching. Theeey Ring Mr. Ching.

Remember, for delicious Chinese food delivered right to your doorstep, just [telephone sound effect] Ring Mr. Ching."

The word "ching" is in this sixty-second radio spot twenty-four times. I will give you one guess as to what happened every time we ran those radio spots. Mr. Ching's phones rang off the hook. And that was years before car phones. Prospects had to remember to Ring Mr. Ching after they arrived home. No telling what would have happened if they could have called from their cars.

Mr. Ching delivered the highest sales per deliverable household in the history of Chinese food.

And had our secret corporate investor not decided to get out of the Chinese restaurant business even after this success, you would probably be ringing Mr. Ching in your own neighborhood by now.

We closed Mr. Ching a little over ten years ago. I will meet people at cocktail parties who used to live near one, and when they find out what I do, they will repeat this Mr. Ching advertising almost word for word. They claim that it irritated them, but they remember it.

Linkage is so important that you can have only a so-so core expectation when it comes to a compelling differentiation, but if you get everything perfectly aligned against that expectation and then execute great linkage, you can still create a Killer Brand. The following is a good example.

BRAND STUDY: Shout It Out!!

It was 1972. Texize, that Janitor in a Drum company, had just created a new spray laundry stain-remover category with its new Spray 'n Wash brand. SC Johnson (Johnson Wax), the second company in the category, wanted to be the market leader in this new category because market research showed that it could grow significantly. The category at the time was about $15 million and growing about 20 percent a year.

Johnson Wax Research & Development was charged with creating a formula that would test with consumers as superior to Spray 'n Wash. The target guideline was a 60 percent to 40 percent preference over Spray 'n Wash in side-by-side, in-home consumer use testing.

Try as they might, SC Johnson could only get to a 53 percent to 47 percent winner. What to do? This is one of those situations where great marketing can kick in and save the day. A 53 percent to 47 percent winner did not meet SC Johnson's internal guidelines for the introduction of new brand, and it was hardly a landslide endorsement of a new formula. But the product did get out a few stains that nothing else would, particularly greasy stains, so the new brand moved forward.

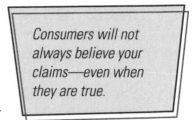

Consumers will not always believe your claims—even when they are true.

The brand was originally called Capture and even the name Shanghai was considered. The idea was that this formula penetrated your fabric and literally kidnapped stains.

Neither of these names tested well and one was not trademarkable. The situation worsened. The company had a mildly superior formula and no name. Test market was already scheduled. Into the company's treasure trove of owned trademarks the brand team dived. It turned out that SC Johnson had tested unsuccessfully a floor cleaner in the 1950s under the name **Shout,** and the company still owned the trademark.

The Shout name sounded strong and efficacious to consumers in research, so Shout it became.

During simulated test markets, it became clear that consumers did not believe any of Shout's advertising. They did not believe the claims. Years and years of advertising for detergents and other laundry additives had dulled their senses to any brand's performance claims. They were jaundiced. They did not believe anything. Even powerful side-by-side demos were ignored or disbelieved.

Envision the situation. Shout had an iffy superiority, a brand name borrowed from another project (which had failed), and advertising that was not believable. But the category was still enticing. The company thought the category could grow to at least $50 million with another strong competitor. But SC Johnson also wanted leadership, and Spray 'n Wash was becoming more entrenched by the day.

A Brand Backbone Strategy was developed that called for the following basic marketing strategy. "Use introductory marketing to accelerate category growth and seize leadership by gaining a disproportionate share of new uses." The plan was to send direct samples to 19.2 million households. We merged and purged a list from twenty-six characteristics that correlated to heavy laundry usage. Number one was "drives a station wagon." Testing showed that our resulting mailing list was almost 70 percent heavy launderers (sixteen loads a week). A normal list of representative households would have only included 44 per cent heavy launderers. We intended to use highly memorable frequent advertising to cause sample usage, conversion to purchase, and habit formation.

Thus we wanted a memorable idea for Shout. We started working on ways to rhyme Shout with out. You would think in retrospect that this would have been easy. You would think wrong.

In test markets, we were using the phrase, "Tough stains come out when you spray on Shout." It was good, but not great advertising.

The ad agency Foote, Cone & Belding came in one day with a storyboard that featured a husband sheepishly approaching his wife at the washer with a shirt that he had soiled badly. He offered to clean it himself if his wife would show him how. She took one look and said, "Just Shout it out."

He did as she said. He started hollering at his shirt. She said "No, silly," and grabbed the shirt, introduced the brand, sprayed the stain, and of course the shirt came clean. The spot ended with the husband in a clean shirt, and the announcer saying, "When you want a tough stain out, Shout it out!"

We told the agency that "Shout It Out" was it. That was the slogan we had been looking for because it was both memorable and behavioral. Remember, we were trying to add category users and stimulate new behavior to build the category. We added that we were not sure that the execution with the husband was the best they could do, so we sent them back to Chicago with marching orders to create new executions of Shout It Out advertising. Four weeks later we had seen none.

The brand team and the creative director, Patrick Derby, were in Pasadena at the home of John Chulay, associate producer of *The Mary Tyler Moore Show*. We had rented his house for the day and were using it to shoot another commercial in the "tough stains come out when you spray on Shout" campaign.

During a break I asked Patrick, "What ever came of the Shout It Out idea? Why haven't we seen more executions on the idea?"

He replied candidly that Arthur Shultz (CEO of Foote, Cone at the time) didn't like it, thought that it was in poor taste, and that Sam Johnson (CEO and sole owner of SC Johnson) wouldn't like it, so he killed it. I was young then, and thought I was much better than I was. Thus my ire was easily aroused. In fact, I grew livid.

"Well, Arthur Shultz is not working on this brand, and Sam Johnson is not part of this brand group. We want Shout It Out advertising and we want it now!"

Patrick Derby and I then went out back to the kid's sand-box, and using scenes that we were shooting for the "tough stains come out when you spray on Shout" ad, wrote a new ad featuring the mom saying, "I'd Shout It Out!" four times. We paid the talent extra to stay after the shoot to film the four "Shout It Out" lines.

The next day Pat Derby and I went to an editing lab with the footage and cut ourselves a "Shout It Out" ad. We then on-air tested this new advertising without gaining permission of any higher-ups at SC Johnson or at Foote, Cone & Belding. We did not even tell them until after the fact.

This new "Shout It Out" ad tested well and ended up doing the job for Shout in the market. We zoomed to category leadership. The category growth exploded. Shout scored the highest unaided brand awareness that I had ever seen at the time, and 52 percent of the target audience had unaided recall of the "Shout It Out" line itself. Unaided recall, by the way, is giving the answer to "What laundry stain removers can you think of?" Aided recall is: "Have you ever heard of Shout?" In this case, when asked what laundry advertising can you think of, 52 percent of the target audience replied Shout and remembered the slogan, "Shout it out!" on an unaided basis.

I am not sure if Sam Johnson liked the "Shout It Out" advertising, nor am I sure that Arthur Shultz ever changed his mind. But neither ever complained.

Today, over thirty years later, Shout is an $800 million global brand for SC Johnson, and the brand's slogan is still "Shout It Out."

Is Shout a Killer Brand? Not quite because its formulas have never had the superior margin of preference that a Killer Brand has, but it sure got its alignment and linkage down correctly.

Fast and Effective Linkage

There are plenty of other great linking examples. "Never wear black without the blue" for **Selsun Blue** dandruff shampoo. "Dirt can't hide from intensified Tide" for Tide XK. "Let a little **Sun-In** put a little fun in your hair" for Sun-In hair lightener. I could go on forever.

What I want you to take away from this is that your messages should and can link to the core expectation of your brand no matter what your brand is named. The weaker the linkage, the more you will have to spend on advertising to create a marketplace effect and the more ads you will need to buy. The stronger your linkage, the faster you will build the effect, and theoretically the less you will need to spend, the fewer ads you will need to buy.

Isn't it interesting that for most of the history of advertising agencies their financial compensation was greater when you spent more money buying more ads? I don't want to accuse anyone, but for a hundred years before the fee systems started coming around, it was not in an ad agency's financial best interest to create advertising that was so good at linkage that you could spend less on it.

11

Keep It Simple and Clear

"Shout It Out," "You'll wonder where the yellow went when you brush your teeth with Pepsodent," and "Ring Mr. Ching" are simple, and they are clear. This is what you are going for.

Let's look at a few more examples of clarity. The first involves peanut butter and a phrase that managed to stick to the tip of nearly everyone's tongue.

BRAND STUDY: Choosy Mothers Choose Jif

Jif was first introduced in 1958 when market leadership in the peanut butter category was a hard-fought battle between Skippy and Peter Pan. Jif was introduced only as a creamy style. Jif caught on early with adults and kids because of its distinct taste profile that consumers reported tasted more like fresh peanuts. In fact, Jif tastes more like fresh peanuts than it would if you yourself ground fresh peanuts into peanut butter. I know because I have conducted this experiment. You can tell that I am a Jif fan, but just of the creamy!

Jif added a crunchy style in 1971, then Simply Jif with reduced sodium and other variations later. The Jif brand was sold by Procter & Gamble to the Smucker's company in 2001.

Jif represents the amazing staying power of a compelling differentiation (tastes more like fresh peanuts) combined with great brand name linkage ("Choosy Mothers Choose Jif"). This campaign, while not around immediately when the brand was introduced, is credited with eventually building the brand's leadership, and the campaign format and the slogan (not a tag line, but a legitimate slogan) have now been on the air for decades.

It is very rare in my experience for a company to acquire even a leading brand from another, much less keep the advertising without changing it. Of course that is exactly what Smucker's should be doing, but it is rare that they are actually doing it and keeping the brand consistency that has meant so much to consumers over the years.

Two new commercials have aired recently with slightly modified formats, but they are still in the same time-tested campaign. The first features two tween girls at a pajama party when they decide to fix peanut butter sandwiches. They get all excited to find that their mothers both cut the bread across when preparing sandwiches and the slogan "Choosy

Moms Choose Jif," a slight modernization of the original, is still used.

A second commercial features a dad fixing a peanut butter sandwich for his daughter. They enjoy their Jif together and a slightly different slogan is used, "Choosy Moms, and Dads, Choose Jif."

I personally don't care for this change. If the changing makeup of the American household means that Choosy Moms Choose Jif should be modified, I believe I might have changed it to Choosy Parents Choose Jif to maintain the meter of the original slogan.

But this decision is clearly testable, which I am sure they must have done. So don't pay as much attention to my opinion on the slogan change as to the fact that for decades this brand has achieved and maintained market leadership by maintaining great consistency, dependability, and stability.

And because they landed on a compelling differentiation, aligned to it, figured out how to make it theirs, and linked well enough to their brand name, they became, and continue to be, a Killer Brand.

Just in case you are thinking that the principle of linkage applies only to TV-advertised brands, let's discuss a few brands that built this linkage right into their names, packaging, and in-store materials because they knew that the idea was not big enough to warrant big-time media investments.

BRAND STUDY: A Cough Drop with a Clear Message

Have you ever been in a fishing boat on a cold wet morning waiting for something to happen? Have you ever been out to sea on a wet, windy day? Can you imagine your being in either scenario from the lazy comfort of the recliner in your great room?

If you were in a boat on a wet, windy, raw day, what would your throat feel like? How would your sinuses react to the situation and to the weather? Would the taste and effect of a cough drop feel good?

Now let's transfer ourselves to a store. If you saw a cough drop named **Fisherman's Friend** with a man in a slicker on the package standing behind the wheel of a sailing vessel trying to navigate through wind and waves, what expectation do you develop immediately for that cough drop?

Would it be strong or mild? Would it have a nice flavor or would it taste more like medicine? Would it be mostly flavor and soothing, or would it have a jolt of sinus-opening effect?

Are there circumstances when you think it might be the best cough drop for you?

I think that Fisherman's Friend cough drops are one of the best-organized little non-advertised brands in the store. It is generally an in-and-out brand, with the stores choosing to carry it only during the cold season and buy it only in floor stands rather than add it to the shelves.

The issue in becoming a Killer Brand is not how big you can be, but how compelling you can be, how "best" you can be. It is this clear and compelling differentiation that allows you to maximize profit return at any sales level, be it under $10 million or over $1 billion.

I personally would love to own Fisherman's Friend. With this one small in-and-out brand, you and your family could build a net worth in the millions.

The permission to believe in the Fisherman's Friend concept is very close to the Norwegian Formula hand cream that I had at Neutrogena, "developed for the hands of Norwegian fisherman so think what it could do for you."

And the relevance in the Fisherman's Friend concept is also close to another very successful concept in the marketplace, one of the leading flavors in tea bags, **Constant Comment** tea. Constant Comment is just an orange pekoe tea differentiated in a nice, clear way. Think of tea-drinking moments. You are either alone and pensive, or you are with a single friend or small group of friends. One hardly ever drinks hot tea in large groups of people. The idea of your cup of tea providing companionship and a Constant Comment is heartwarming, and isn't that what tea is about?

You don't have to own a giant business to benefit from owning a Killer Brand.

The following is another small brand that I would love to own. It is in an entirely different category from Fisherman's Friend although I can imagine them displayed in a drug store or in a home center with the two displays within eyesight of each other.

BRAND STUDY: A Clean Sweep

I was walking through a Home Depot one day and saw this adorable little character cutting its eyes up at me as I walked by. It was a cardboard face surrounding a round, ball-like head on the end of a telescoping handle. In fact there was a little crowd of them with their handles (bodies) gathered into a round, trashcan-like display.

It was the face of **Webster,** a cleaning device for getting rid of spider webs. The head was designed to trap webs and let you kind of twist the web completely in. The telescoping handle extended to twenty feet or more. This seemed like a good idea for me. We have several very high ceilings in our house and spider webs are sometimes trouble in places that we cannot reach.

There was well-organized instant equity and understanding in this brand, although I had never seen it advertised or seen anything like it.

My immediate expectation was compelling. I could use Webster to get down spider webs without getting the ladders out. Everything about the product looked as if it would work well for its intended use. It was priced fairly, about $7.99, which was high enough for me to believe that it really worked and low enough to be preferable to the ladder routine. And the personification of the Webster face on the packaging around the head of the product linked the brand to its expectation much better than if it had been called "telescoping handle spider-web remover."

I am relatively certain that I would not have noticed this product had it been generically labeled. But those big eyes looking up at me from Webster's head did it instantly. I bought three Websters, one for my house, one for my office, and one for my mother's house.

Webster was not a perfect business proposition. Once you had one, you probably would not need another one for the rest of your life. There was no replacement part so no continuing revenue. So it would be difficult for most people to qualify Webster as a Killer Brand, but within its own set of competition, brooms and such, I believe that it was.

They managed to sell millions of Websters with no advertising and no discount pricing.

Now lest you think this principle of linkage applies only to national brands, whether they are advertised or not, let's examine a few local businesses that have accomplished the same, but within a limited geographic area. The first is a window-blind installation company and the last two are regional meatpackers.

BRAND STUDY: Can You See the Linkage?

I am driving down the highway in either Denver or Salt Lake City and am passed by a white van painted with the silhouette of a man wearing dark glasses. On it is the logo for **The Blind Man,** a company that sells and installs window blinds.

Besides the attention-grabbing and memory-sticking properties of the name, there is, I believe, a subliminal expectation of privacy in this name. So instead of wondering how a blind man could put up my blinds correctly, my mind goes to a blind man as the perfect person to put up my blinds. I also think that I could close the blinds at any time for personal privacy to become blind to the world.

I know that my added perception in this case may seem to be a stretch, but I believe that the linkage and subliminal promise or expectation in The Blind Man name is one of the factors that has led this business to be such a successful and quickly expanding franchise.

Is the name The Blind Man politically correct? Probably not, but my immediate reaction in my car that day was "Why didn't I think of that?"

One of the advantages in traveling as much as I do, both domestically and internationally, is that I get to see a lot of brand efforts by a lot of smart individuals and companies to which I would never be exposed if I were stationary in my Atlanta office. Not only do I get to visit with them in my consulting practice, but more importantly I am exposed to them driving down highways, walking by storefronts, and going into stores and shopping.

The next example is one that I happened upon very early in my career, so long ago that this brand no longer exists, having been absorbed in one or more mergers or acquisitions.

BRAND STUDY: The Keener Wiener

In 1968 when I was a brand assistant on **White Cloud** toilet tissue at Procter & Gamble, I was sent to Youngstown, Ohio, on my first "store check." A store check is when you go to a local market and drive around all day and actually go into stores unannounced and check on brand availability, shelf space and placement, pricing, competitive offers, promotional support, etc. If you do a store check correctly, you also talk to the manager and the person in charge of working your section. Your objective is to learn firsthand as much as you can about your brand in that particular market and just get a feel for the real world.

Interestingly, I was excited about this trip for two reasons. First, it was my first store check on my own. Second, it was in Youngstown, Ohio, which was the home of Frankie Sinkwich, the only Heisman Trophy winner at that time from the University of Georgia, my alma mater.

Even more interesting when it comes to the principle of Linkage, I only remember two things about that first store check and neither of them has anything to do with my assigned brand at that time. I remember the sign at the city limits announcing that Youngstown was indeed the home of the great Frankie Sinkwich. And I remember a billboard for a local hot dog brand, **Keener.**

Keener, as I learned at the time, marketed itself as the brand of hot dog that did not use spare remnant parts like ground-up bones, chicken wings, beaks, etc. in their hot dogs—implying, of course, that other brands of hot dogs did.

Here was the slogan on their billboard, "Keener, the Cleaner Wiener."

I drove by this billboard exactly once. I happened to hear the story explained in a radio ad that day that talked about the purity of ingredients in Keener wieners. I have never heard of this brand again in almost forty years. If I saw it on the shelf today, I would still buy it because of the expectation that I would be buying and eating a purer hot dog.

In the case of Keener, I am a prospect with a message frequency of only two in one day. I had never seen advertising for this product before, nor did I see any afterwards, but the expectation was so compelling and so differentiated and so linked to the brand name that I have never forgotten it after forty years. Most of the time, we cannot even remember advertising we were exposed to an hour ago.

I cannot confirm that this brand or company still exists (many regional meatpackers have merged over the last forty years), but I did give a presentation at the Goodyear Rubber company recently in Akron, Ohio, and some of the older people there still remembered the Keener company.

Talk about staying power, "Keener, the Cleaner Wiener."

I spoke of Drew Fagan earlier as one of my favorite creative people of all time. Another is Marian Dawson. Marian is originally from Mobile, Alabama, but spent his entire career in advertising in Chicago, at Leo Burnett and Needham, Harper & Steers among other agencies. I credit Marian with "I wish I were an **Oscar Mayer** wiener," **McDonald's** "You deserve a break today," and **State Farm's** "Like a good neighbor, State Farm is there."

But two of my favorite Marian Dawson campaigns were for very small companies that you may never have heard of. The first is for a regional meatpacker in Oklahoma City. Marian did this campaign after founding his own agency, Dawson, Johns & Black, with two associates from his days at Leo Burnett.

BRAND STUDY: Joe Mahoney Baloney

The scene opens on a father sitting with his son next to a campfire. Son is about 8 or 9 years old. He is having a baloney sandwich and obviously really enjoying it.

"Son, you really love that **Joe Mahoney Baloney,** don't you?" Son nods because mouth is full. "You know, when I was your age I went to school with Joe Mahoney. He was a neat kid. Joe Mahoney loved baloney more than anything else in the world. He used to say to us, 'When I grow up I am going to make the best baloney in the world. To start with I am going to make it square to fit the bread.'" Son's eyes grow wide in admiration for Joe Mahoney and for his dad. The announcer comes in: "Joe Mahoney Baloney, square so it fits the bread."

Is there focus in this message? Is there a brand expectation that is differentiated? Is that difference likely to be compelling to the target audience? Is there linkage between the focus and the brand name? Does anything seem to be out of alignment? (Of course you cannot tell that from just this one commercial.)

One important thing to know here is that Joe Mahoney Baloney was a new product. The meatpacking company was not called Joe Mahoney. Joe is a fictional character made up to create a branded difference in what is traditionally a commodity-type category.

I have always loved this example because it shows what brilliant things can happen when you combine good Killer Brand principles with great messaging. The whole idea that Joe Mahoney started thinking about creating the world's best baloney when he was a kid about the same age as the target audience just nails it. It works. We should all be so lucky in our brand efforts.

While we are discussing linkage, it would be helpful to return to the Duracell versus Energizer example that we looked at back in the chapter on Expectation, because both brands have executed the principle of linkage rather brilliantly.

BRAND STUDY: The Copper-Top Bunny

The battery business is a real battle between two Killer Brands, Duracell and Energizer.

Duracell created linkage by creating a packaging difference along with a mnemonic (memory) device in its advertising to link its promise of durability and performance to its brand, not just to its brand name. In doing so, it actually created linkage on it package.

The band of copper around the top of each battery was referred to in the advertising as the "copper top." Advertising shows the copper top folding down on the Duracell battery as if a lid is closing, and a sound effect accompanies the closing at the same time, thus creating a memory device for the copper top that is concept, sound, and visual, the visual then being replicated on the package in the store. This is brilliant linkage.

Eveready, eventually renamed Energizer, struggled for years to compete with this excellent Duracell advertising and linkage until finally the **Energizer Bunny** was born.

What does the Energizer Bunny do? "It keeps going and going and going!" What is the compelling expectation that drives choice in the battery business? The expectation is that it will last a long time. What is the linkage? It's the Energizer Bunny, not just any bunny.

The Energizer Bunny is designed to resemble the brand, as is the drum that it beats. Eventually, the brand actually added the bunny to the brand's packaging, but that is a move that you generally should not pursue unless you know you have an idea that is going to work and that you are going to stick with for a long time, at least five years. If every brand changed their packaging every time they changed their advertising, the world of brands would be even more confusing.

It is rare that two major brands in a category will both have such excellent linkage and long-lasting campaigns, but this side-by-side battle in batteries has sure made it difficult for a third brand to emerge, hasn't it? The category is a multi-billion-dollar business and there is sure room for more than two major brands, but the two that dominate the category have so many of the Killer Brand principles going for them that there is no room for any other brand to make a big move.

This kind of dominance through principle is the advantage of Killer Branding.

12

Reinforce Linkage at Every Chance

To create a Killer Brand, you can't use Linkage as simply a one-time strategy. In this chapter, we'll look at several examples of companies that have creatively and persistently used linkage to make their brands much more powerful.

BRAND STUDY: It's Hard to Stop a Trane

I absolutely love what **Trane** has been doing. I own three different central air conditioning units in my current home and they certainly have their share of problems, it seems every year.

I had to replace a unit lately and I chose Trane. In fact, I forced my HVAC supplier to use a Trane. He tried to convince me that a Trane unit was not worth the extra 12 percent it cost versus the similar Carrier unit.

But I believe in brands so I went for Trane. They have told me that "It's hard to stop a Trane" so many times and in so many ways—in ads, on trucks, on uniforms, on billboards, over the radio, etc.—that, frankly, I believe it.

Because I was working on this book, I actually contacted the company to see how much evidence exists to support my expectation that if I buy a Trane it is going to last longer.

They chose not to respond. That doesn't inspire my confidence. Does it work for you?

The following company, however, is about as responsive as a company can get.

BRAND STUDY: Eat Mor Chikin

Chick-fil-A is the second largest chicken fast-food restaurant chain in America with revenues just short of $2 billion. Its beginnings go all the way back to the founder S. Truett Cathy opening the Dwarf Grill in 1946 in Hapeville, Georgia.

But what we want to review here in this book is their current advertising and their brand slogan, which is such a good example of the principle of linkage.

Since an initial billboard in 1994, the Chick-fil-A advertising features cows in all kinds of different situations imploring us, the target audience, to "EAT MOR CHIKIN." This brand slogan is generally communicated to us via handwritten signs around the cows' necks. The misspellings, of course, come from the cows.

Chick-fil-A's logic is based on the belief that if America eats less beef and more chicken, Chick-fil-A will gain business. I think the cows are actually a better idea than that.

Implicit in the Chick-fil-A brand is the notion that it is good for you to eat more chicken and less beef. Using the principles in this book, what is the focus of Chick-fil-A? The focus is "eating chicken," isn't it? Does Chick-fil-A stay on focus? Absolutely, they do. They neither sell nor advertise anything that is not made from chicken, much to the relief of the cows.

What is the brand expectation that drives users to eat more chicken? I believe this campaign works best among the audience that already knows about Chick-fil-A and has experienced the products there. They remember via the frequency of the message and the slogan how much they enjoy Chick-fil-A. I believe that the cows are what makes this slogan work and what makes it memorable at all. If Chick-fil-A told us to "eat more chicken" with absolutely the same frequency of messaging but without the consistency of the cows, I don't think that even the linkage would work so well.

The retail food business is very interesting in that a broad spectrum of the prospect base is in the market to buy every day, many of them several times each day. Therefore, top-of-mind awareness can actually work to drive brand usage. Enter linkage and frequency of messaging and that is what the Chick-fil-A cows do.

Every ad features the cows. Every ad, no matter the medium, features the slogan, "EAT MOR CHIKIN." Visual mediums deliver the slogan generally through cow-worn signs. Radio, of course, does not.

The Chick-fil-A cows are so famous that they have been inducted into the Advertising Hall of Fame.

Remember Marian Dawson of Joe Mahoney fame? Here is another of my favorite brand stories, one that was also produced by his brilliant mind.

BRAND STUDY: Rusty Jones

There once was a small $2 million automobile rustproofing company outside of Chicago. It was named Body by Thixotex. It claimed to have superior products and service to the market leader at the time, **Ziebart**.

The owner of Body by Thixotex wanted Marian Dawson and his advertising agency Dawson, Johns & Black to take him on as an account even though he was very small, way too small in fact to be a viable account for the agency.

Marian decided to do it, but only if the owner of the company would let them reinvent the brand. In this case, the technology and product seemed sound. The company could support its claims of superiority over Ziebart. But even the great Marian Dawson did not think he could create a well-known brand out of Body by Thixotex.

The brand was reinvented as **Rusty Jones.** Advertising created a cartoon character that resembled Jim Black, an art director and one of the founders of the agency. This Rusty Jones cartoon character was larger than life and rode on every car that was protected by Rusty Jones.

Within two rust seasons, Rusty Jones had grown to over $100 million in sales. Unfortunately, the market changed when manufacturers started rustproofing every car as part of the new-car process. Eventually the rustproofing aftermarket went away, but the category's demise does not stop Rusty Jones from being one incredible example of how important linkage can be for an otherwise very compelling promise for car owners in the upper Midwest with snow and salt on the roads. From $2 million to $100 million in two seasons! I have always been impressed by the accomplishment of Rusty Jones.

I think we mentioned that politicians could be branded. There is a strong example of linkage with both of the gubernatorial candidates in the state of Georgia for 2006.

Sonny Do and the Big Guy

The two candidates in Georgia in 2006 were Sonny Perdue, the incumbent governor, and Mark Taylor, the challenger.

Mark Taylor is a very tall, very large man—I would estimate in excess of 300 pounds. He was the lieutenant governor running to unseat his boss, the current governor.

Mark Taylor calls himself the Big Guy, and he was running for the Little Guy. It is pretty impossible not to remember this advertising and get a fairly clear message of a liberal politician who believes in the government taking care of the little guy. Good linkage.

But Sonny was the current governor and had a list of accomplishments that had occurred during his term. His campaign revolved around the expectation that he will get things done. His campaign slogan is "Sonny Did"; nothing mind-blowing there, but here is the big idea.

His campaign folks have created a "Sonny Do" list with advertising, testimonials, and a Web site where you can write your own suggestion to Sonny. Someone replies to each suggestion and every one that results in a gubernatorial action or a piece of recommended legislature is heavily advertised as part of the "Sonny Do" list.

To make things even more consistent with the well-known concept of a "Honeydew" or "Honey Do" list, the governor's wife came on the air every now and then and added to his "Sonny Do" list. I think this "Sonny Do" list is a brilliant brand-marketing idea. Hats off to whoever created it.

It is compelling, differentiated, aligned to the balance of his campaign and record, and linked memorably to his name, Sonny Perdue. Political campaign ideas do not get any better than the "Sonny Do" list.

In the November 2006 election, Sonny Perdue coasted to his second term as governor of Georgia.

BRAND STUDY: Tony the Tiger

Tony the Tiger, the mascot of **Kellogg's Frosted Flakes**, made his first appearance in 1952. He was designed by children's book illustrator Martin Provensen and his voice was provided by Dallas McKennon. He was originally one of several mascots test-marketed for the product, and quickly became the most popular.

Still in his early days, Tony was given a son, Tony Junior, and a new voice, provided by Thurl Ravenscroft. In the 1970s, Kellogg's unsuccessfully attempted to interest consumers in the rest of Tony's family: Mama Tony, Mrs. Tony, and daughter Antoinette. Son Tony Junior was given his own product, **Frosted Rice.** (You are savvy enough by now to know why this was not a good idea.)

In 2005, Thurl Ravenscroft died and Kellogg's signed a ten-year contract with Lee Marshall, formerly a wrestling announcer, to be the new voice of Tony.

In an interesting compromise between brand consistency and keeping up with the times, the original Tony has morphed over the years from a whimsical, rather simply drawn creature to a bigger, stronger, muscular mascot more appropriate to today's values. Frosted Flakes have changed a little also, but we are still reminded over and over that "They're Grrreat!"

PART FIVE

WHAT TO DO—AND WHAT NOT TO DO

13

Don't Confuse Your Prospects

I am trying diligently to make the principles in this book clear, particularly since there are two background assertions concerning Choice and Expectation, and then three actual principles (Focus, Alignment, and Linkage) for creating and sustaining a Killer Brand.

And I have had a lot of time with my prospect—you, the reader. You are investing hours of your valuable time in reading this book and making the principles your own. Think about how much more difficult it would be for me to burn in these principles talking with each of you once or twice a week for thirty seconds each time, for about twelve to twenty talks in total.

That is what you are facing with your own sales prospects, or worse. That is why you must be clear and simple and why you absolutely cannot confuse your prospects.

BRAND STUDY: But He Can't Swim

There is a very nice bit of drama on television at the moment disguised as advertising. It is brilliantly shot and produced, with great casting and scenery. The time period for the ad is the Middle Ages. The location is obviously in Europe in a small village somewhere.

In the middle of a bridge that spans a river, a man stands on the edge, wearing a set of wings strapped to his arms. He has drawn a crowd and is obviously quite nervous about his upcoming experiment with flight. It is very clear that he is going to jump off the bridge wearing his flying apparatus.

Okay, I will interject a question here. What brand do you think is being advertised here? No idea, right?

Now back to the ad.

The man teeters on the edge of the bridge. Nervous twitters ripple through the audience of villagers who have joined the onlookers. Suddenly the man dives off of the bridge and begins to slowly but powerfully flap the wings that are strapped to his arms. After he loses a little altitude, the wind catches under the wings and he begins to fly, albeit very briefly.

The audience is stunned. "He can fly. He can fly," one after another exclaims. But as he loses a little altitude and gets closer and closer to the water, one man on the end of the bridge says, "Yes, but he cannot swim." Our flier then hits the water, wings and all.

Twenty-eight of the thirty seconds have passed. What product do you think this ad is for?

I am going to leave you to figure this out yourself. What could it be? As I finished writing this case, I realized that I was not so sure myself what this commercial was advertising even though I have seen it and enjoyed it at least a dozen times. I did not want to be wrong in the book, so I decided to

just let you think about it. Read this example again and you tell me what this ad is supposed to be selling.
What is the expectation? What is the brand?

The next case is about a product that I have loved for almost my entire career as an example of Killer Brand principles—until just recently. Let's take a thorough look.

BRAND STUDY: It's Raining Gatorade?

For most of its life, **Gatorade** has been a Killer Brand. As with many great brands, the creator was not a professional marketer. He was a doctor taking care of athletes at the University of Florida.

If you have ever been in Gainesville, Florida, you know how hot and humid it can get there. Imagine being on the football team in Gainesville, or playing any other sport that requires physically grueling outdoor exercise there.

In Gainesville, you sweat with a capital S. It pours out of you. Some players can lose as much as eleven pounds in one practice.

Back in the early 1960s, it was discovered that water just was not enough to rehydrate players while they were practicing. So the team physician developed a drink with electrolytes and balanced carbohydrates in the hope that he could produce a rehydrating liquid that would be absorbed by the body more rapidly than water.

He called it Gatorade because it came to the aid of players on the various Florida Gator teams. I was first given this miracle elixir in 1963 while playing tennis there.

Gatorade continued to be used only at the University of Florida until it was licensed by the Stokely-Van Camp company and introduced as the market's first isotonic beverage.

During its ownership by Stokely, Gatorade established itself slowly and grew, but not to giant status.

Then the Quaker company acquired Stokely, mainly to get Gatorade. They also kept the Van Camp's canned business.

Someone at Quaker figured out that exercise, amateur sports, and fitness had been on the rise for a long time in America, and that the brand's origins as developed for real athletes was an important part of the brand expectation into the future.

Quaker invested aggressively in the growth of Gatorade with a lot of team sponsorships to ensure "sideline" exposure of the brand during college and professional sports, as well as with distribution, promotion, and advertising.

Soon the brand, which was really also the category at the time, was over $600 million. This was too large for the soft-drink giants to ignore, and Coca-Cola introduced **Powerade** at about the same time that Pepsi introduced **All Sport**. During the introduction of these two competing brands, the category zoomed and Gatorade's incremental volume during the introductory years of the two competitors was greater than either of the two brands' volume. In other words, Gatorade was a Killer Brand, and grew faster during the competitive introductions than they did before the competitors were there.

When I last checked in on Gatorade personally (they were a client for many of these years), the brand was pushing $2 billion worldwide and was still owned by Quaker.

The fallout from all of this was that Pepsi decided to acquire Gatorade instead of compete with them, and the brand transferred a few years ago.

For almost forty years Gatorade kept its core brand expectation the same: rehydration. The brand stayed on the same strategy for all that time. It was all about rehydration at the "point of sweat."

Now Gatorade has introduced **Propel,** a fitness water, which I kind of understand as a consumer. But they have also introduced Gatorade Rain. I have no idea as a consumer what Gatorade Rain is and how it compares to Gatorade.

There has never been a single day in my life since 1963 that I did not know exactly what Gatorade was and exactly when I should drink it. I understood the product positioning. I understood the usage positioning. I understood the personal positioning.

I have watched Peyton Manning burst up through a rubber body suit advertising Gatorade Rain at least fifty times, and I still don't know what the brand is and/or what I should expect from it.

I will accept that it is possible that I am the only consumer in the world confused by Gatorade Rain. But I would offer even money that I am not.

Here is another brand idea that I see on the TV a lot right now that is confusing to me. In fact, it makes no sense.

BRAND STUDY: Cut Out the Scissors, Please

I know what **Discover Card** is. I know it was developed and introduced originally by Sears. I know that the core brand expectation is a rebate at the end of the year equal to one percent of every dollar you charge on it. In my mind the Discover Card is down the line on the pecking order for charge card status, with American Express on the top, Master Card and Visa neck and neck in second position, and Discover Card last.

Now I keep seeing these commercials with scissors coming up out of the street and out of cars and tables and everything. Even with computer animation, these ads must have cost millions to produce, and even more to run. I see them everywhere. To their minimum credit, I do know that these ads are for the Discover Card, but I have absolutely no idea what they say or what I am supposed to make of them.

To say that I am confused by the Discover Card ads is an understatement. I suspect strongly that I am technically in their target audience because I sure run a lot of money through charge cards each month.

They are not going to develop me as a customer with communications that just confuse me. Not only are they making me think, which we have agreed is not in their best interest, they are prohibiting me from thinking accurately. Wow!

Sometimes when a brand is confusing enough, it does not stay in business. The following sad story is about an airline that flew back and forth from Los Angeles to New York.

BRAND STUDY: Which Audience to Target?

Regent Air was conceived as better than first class, almost like having your own corporate jet to fly on. It was different from the current time-share programs like **Net Jets.** On Regent Air, you flew in an absolutely luxurious plane with fabulous service any time you wished, with no prearranged commitment of fees. You purchased each ticket individually just as you would on any commercial airline, just at about a 60 percent premium over first-class commercial.

Good market research showed two significant target audiences, each of which found this concept very appealing. The first was the Hollywood film set, few of whom had private planes at their disposal. The second was corporate executives and successful business owners who did not yet have private planes at their disposal.

What could possibly be confusing about this concept?

The Hollywood crew expected the plane to be filled with other film people. The corporate crew expected the plane to be filled with other executives. The two groups proved to have quite incompatible expectations.

The Hollywood crew liked to party a little in the air, and often showed up with recreational assistance. The corporate crowd liked to work or rest on the plane. They showed up with stuffed briefcases and *Wall Street Journal*s. Within the confines of a small private-type jet, these two audiences were like oil and water.

Hollywood was confused. The corporate target was confused. The business was well-funded, but refused to take sides and decide which audience it should target. Regent Air failed against its original objective. It now survives as a small luxury charter service out of Lake Tahoe, California.

This next example is very disappointing to me personally because it tells the story of the rise of a true Killer Brand based on the courage and derring-do of its founder, Ted Turner, followed by its staggering, at the very least.

BRAND STUDY: The Rise and Fall of CNN

CNN was the first all-news channel on broadcast or on cable television. Ted Turner was convinced that a market existed for twenty-four-hour news, and that the market was worldwide. He further was committed to its success.

CNN's core expectation was clear, it was compelling, and it was differentiated.

The CNN brand was so well aligned, and structured so clearly to each of its employees, that the network actually created and aired news on the fly. CNN reporters knew what should be and should not be on the air. They created news

179

reports without supervision or approval. In that way, news was fast and unfettered by hesitation.

When Ted Turner was asked in the thirteenth year of the network why he kept with it even though it was not earning money yet, he replied, "It is important, and if I don't do it, who will?"

In fact, I personally believe that unbiased reporting of the news from CNN did a lot to bring about the dissolution of the Soviet Union. When Gorbachev went to sign the papers to resign as leader of the Soviet Union and the Communist Party, his pen was out of ink, and his press secretary felt in his pockets and found no pen. He turned and borrowed a pen from Tom Johnson, who was the CEO of CNN at the time and standing right behind Gorbachev. After confirming that the pen was a Mt. Blanc and not an American pen, Gorbachev used it, then returned it to Johnson as it was a twenty-fifth anniversary present from Johnson's wife. I think this moment in time was poetic justice, and perhaps the high-water mark of CNN the brand. The papers authorizing the end of the Soviet Union were signed by the personal pen of the CEO of CNN. How symbolic for the world's greatest news organization.

While the brand has not fallen, it certainly has slipped away from the principles that led it to be a Killer Brand. I am not sure whether this is a result of time, or of changed leadership, or of direct competition from **Fox News** and **MSNBC,** or from changed ownership. All I know for sure is that CNN the Killer Brand no longer exists.

Occasionally now I will turn the TV to CNN. I am just as likely to see a feature story about Brad Pitt as I am to see real news. If I wanted to watch *Entertainment Tonight* I would turn to the station that carries that program.

I majored in journalism at the University of Georgia and went to school with Tom Johnson. That's why this particular brand story saddens me so.

Anything Can Be a Brand

You should be getting the sense now from the various examples that we have explored together that anything can be developed as a brand. There is absolutely no product, service, place, building, person—in fact, any choice that cannot be developed as a brand. Even religions are brands, as are celebrities and politicians and political parties, and countries. Is Iran a brand? Does it have a pretty clear message? Is it consistent with that message? Does the brand have the power to affect choices on your behalf when it involves Iran? Sure it does. How many of us are planning to visit Iran on vacation?

The sad thing is that another Muslim country, Morocco, is suffering from brand behavior on the part of several Middle Eastern Muslim countries that are several thousand miles away from Morocco. Tourism in Morocco is down over $10 billion a year since 9/11/2001.

As the following shows, magazines are also good examples of brands.

BRAND STUDY: The Economist

The Economist is a particularly good magazine, in my point of view. Whenever I pick up a copy, I always am well informed by its contents.

The magazine recently started a very aggressive advertising campaign. I have seen many different small billboards for this campaign in airline terminals.

The trouble is that the linkage in this advertising comes only from using a red background for the ads against which the messages, really headlines only, are reversed out. But the big trouble is that there is no consistency whatsoever in the messages. They are all different. I would estimate that I have seen twenty over the last two weeks. Recognize that I have heightened awareness because of the business that I am in, and because I am in the middle of writing this book. I have paid attention because I decided to add this campaign as an example in this book.

Yet I cannot remember a single word from any one of these messages. That is how disjointed they are. The campaign is so confusing that I cannot even remember why I am confused.

This is a clear Killer Brand "no-no"!

The following is an example of an otherwise good brand that seems to be beginning to confuse its users. This conclusion is based on casual interviews that I did for this book with a few of their heavy users as well as personal in-store observations in their stores in a number of different cities.

BRAND STUDY: Losing the "Wow" Factor

Chico's has been an excellent example of a retail clothing store brand that became a Killer Brand in its particular price range and among its very specific target audience.

Chico's targeted over-thirty-five women who could no longer wear the clothes designed and cut for the younger crowd but still wanted to be fashionable. Their signature, according to heavy users who shopped there once or twice a month, was "easy care–easy wear" clothes with an imported feel. The clothes were outside of what the target could find anywhere else.

The alignment between the fashions carried and developed for Chico's, the almost personal-shopper approach of their in-store salespeople, the locations, and the rapidly moving merchandise with new shipments several times a week created a powerfully compelling and differentiated expectation among their early customers. Many became fanatically regular customers, going to Chico's as the store of first choice virtually always before going anywhere else.

As one Chico's devotee explained, "I would wear something from Chico's and people would say 'Wow, where did you buy that?'"

According to these same women, the clothes in Chico's have lost their wow factor. To them, there seems to be much less merchandise in a Chico's store at any given time. The clothing seems to be less differentiated. And it seems to be more similar to what can be found elsewhere. As another Chico's devotee lamented, "The adventure is gone."

I had a woman who works in a mall tell me that she used to stop women who were wearing interesting outfits to ask them where they bought them. About seven out of ten times, she estimated, they answered Chico's. Now she claims that she sees no one to stop and ask.

Interestingly, Chico's same store sales are flat to slightly up, despite their addition of **Soma,** a whole line of lingerie developed for their target audience. All of their growth has been coming from opening new Chico's stores and new stores of their other brands such as **Black Market/White House** and a few standalone Soma stores.

Chico's stock value grew from less than $3.79 in 2001 to a high water mark of $49.40 by February 2006, and has since eroded to $17.80 in the fall of 2006. There appear to be no direct financial causes for the slip in stock value, so it might be due to weakening the perception of the brand, and it might be due to market factors that have nothing to do with Chico's. But, frankly, this erosion occurred during a market run-up. And it happens to be occurring exactly when regular Chico's shoppers are losing some of their zeal for the brand.

14

Now, Put It All Together

We have covered the way the world works based on Choice and Expectation. We have deeply examined the way Killer Brands work based on Focus, Alignment, and Linkage.

Now let's look at some brands that have put it all together. They have managed choices along the chain based on compelling and differentiated expectations. They have followed the principles of Focus, Alignment, and Linkage.

All of them qualify as Killer Brands although the decimal places in the various categories and businesses differ wildly. Some of these brands are worth millions, some are worth hundreds of millions, and a few are worth billions.

A KILLER BRAND IN EIGHTEEN MONTHS

What made the focus of **YouTube** so compelling in eighteen months to drive a startup from a valuation of zero to being purchased by Google for $1.7 billion?

Apparently Andy Warhol was correct when he spoke of every man's fifteen minutes of fame. This Web site, which was differentiated by being set up to accept self-made videos from anyone that could subsequently be viewed by anyone else, made the two young founders very rich very quickly.

All three principles were at work: a simple focus; an aligned strategy and usage characteristics, plus aligned viral marketing; and a memorable enough name and linkage. The result: Startup to $1.7 billion in less than two years.

Here is an example offered because of their ability to create a brand and build a business selling everything at full price and indulging in virtually no bribery-as-substitute-for-marketing.

BRAND STUDY: Bose Follows a Nontraditional Path

Bose is particularly interesting because they have managed to create a Killer Brand in a big category dominated by other companies that went the traditional routes whereas Bose did not.

First of all, the Bose brand is based on differentiated technology, the Bose Wave system, a totally different way to create sound amplification than used for other speakers. The Wave technology always made perfect sense to me because I was once a trombone player. I understood how the simple vibration of my lips could be amplified into a powerful sound by just a few feet of tubing if engineered acoustically well. That's exactly how the Bose Wave system works—a series of acoustically engineered sound chambers through which musical vibrations travel to be amplified.

Second, Bose differentiated itself with its marketing strategy, using ads to create leads and sending salesmen into your home for a demonstration of the Bose Wave machine. They never discounted the $700 price a dime. They generated enough leads with their advertising, and closed enough sales with their in-home demonstrations, to build the company while they worked on even better technology.

Everything that the company did was aligned, including not entering traditional retail sales channels with their technology. They were committed to demonstrations and direct selling. Only recently with their iPod devices have they entered retail, because the target audience is too difficult to reach otherwise.

I have put Bose in this section even though they have really never used language or visuals to create a powerful linkage to their brand. If Bose had a truly great and memorable slogan, they would be an even more powerful brand.

Over the years there have been many good attempts to differentiate tire brands, the most notable in my memory being **Tiger Paws.** But recently, most of the tire manufacturers have seemed content to compete in a commodity-like category with the exception of the following one, which has separated itself from the pack.

BRAND STUDY: Being the Best

Michelin has carved out a unique Killer Brand niche in tires by putting it all together. First there is the focus on superior tires, supported by aligned higher pricing, stronger guarantees, and alignment with top auto manufacturers like Mercedes and others. Virtually every tire dealer I have ever interviewed considers Michelin the best, although there are those who do not consider the difference in quality worth the difference in price. That's fine. Remember, you cannot control the choices of everyone.

Michelin finally worked its way toward an advertising slogan that is aligned with its promise: "Because a lot is riding on your tires."

Michelin is now a good example of getting it all together.

BRAND STUDY: A Successful City Brand

Earlier we examined how Nebraska "buried the lead." Now let's look at a place that has recreated itself as a Killer Brand.

Las Vegas already had the product, and its nickname of "Sin City" did not sit well with city fathers. But when they realized that what visitors really liked about Las Vegas was the freedom to gamble, misbehave, and act like college students, they stumbled upon a great piece of linkage that completed the "Focus–Alignment–Linkage" package for the city brand.

The slogan and idea of "What Happens Here, Stays Here" has helped make Las Vegas one of the most successful city brands of all times.

And finally, I promised to show you a brand that did it all with virtually no resources, just by simply following the rules of "Focus–Alignment–Linkage."

Why Would We Choose the Name "Bullfrog"?

I have saved Bullfrog for last because it represents a case where a lot was accomplished with very few resources. I know this case well because it was likely the high-water mark of my own personal experience in the business of creating a Killer Brand. Never before and never since has everything come together so completely to work so well.

When I left the presidency of Neutrogena I was approached by a local businessman who had come to me in 1980 while I was at Neutrogena to propose the production of a sponsored daily television show on health. This idea was way ahead of cable and way ahead of its time. His name was Don Chelew. His significant other was a nutritionist and together they were a health-crazy couple and wanted to write, produce, and star in the show.

For some reason, I trusted this unknown man off the street and agreed to give him the money to produce sixty-five episodes (thirteen weeks worth of daily shows). We planned to syndicate them to local TV stations around the United States. Neutrogena would have four minutes of advertising on each episode. The broadcast station would have the rest. We decided to use our four minutes to shoot episodes of a skin-care school that featured our products. In 1980, this was perhaps the first example of the infomercials that we know so well today, except that we did not actually sell merchandise during our skin-care schools. I might note that my board of directors thought I had lost my marbles.

Don came through and produced a very credible show, all sixty-five episodes on the very low budget he had proposed. We ran the show in markets around the United States. We shot the episodes as evergreen and ran them over and over. *The Picture of Health*, as it was called, never enjoyed a time slot good enough to give it a chance to generate a rating high enough to measure. We mostly were on early in the morning, most often before 7 A.M. But over two years, Neutrogena sales in markets airing the show averaged a 16 percent gain versus markets without the show. A 2.6 percent increase over one year would have paid out the production cost.

At any rate, the *Picture of Health* experience left me with good vibes about Don Chelew.

Shortly after I left Neutrogena to strike out on my own, the same Don Chelew came to me with an idea for a product. He had a twenty-year-old son, Greg, who already had skin cancer from surfing and being out in the sun too long, and many of Greg's friends already had the same condition. Zinc oxide, the white-nose stuff, had not worked for them.

Don asked me a simple question. "Isn't it possible to create a sunscreen that would stay on in the water?" I told him that I didn't know but we certainly could create a skin-care formula that would not wash off. The issue was whether it would carry a sunscreen compound effectively.

I also doubted that there were enough surfers to drive sufficient brand volume. He explained that the United States alone at that time had 1.4 million surfers. But then he hooked me with this question: "Why can't we use surfers as the torture test for the brand, similar to how you use the Norwegian fishermen as a torture test for Neutrogena Norwegian Formula hand cream?" He was dead right, and a business was born.

The working idea was a water-durable sunscreen. Don was to raise the money, and administer and run the company. I was to run R&D, Sales, and Marketing. We agreed up front that he would share administrative issues with me, but that he could make whatever decision he wished in his areas. I was granted exactly the same deal. We discussed product, sales, and marketing issues, but I had the final call. We arrived at a founder's equity split and started.

We wanted to create a brand to sell to some other company from day one. We never wanted to own the brand any longer than required to get a good price for it. It took about four years. We raised $80,000 the first year, and added another $80,000 the second year. Don, who owned more stock than I did, worked full time. I worked on the brand a few days a month. After four years, we had sales of about $1.6 million with only four employees. We sold and/ or licensed the brand to different companies for a combined price of well over $10 million. We still own the rights in several different countries and are currently developing a new and even bigger idea for the inherent technology.

Here is how we did it.

We determined up front that the differentiated expectation for our brand would be water durability. At that time FDA guidelines stated that a sunscreen that stayed on the skin for twenty minutes in the water was "water resistant" and a sunscreen that stayed on the skin for forty minutes in the water was "waterproof."

> "Cosmetic flaws" help convince a consumer that a product is effective.

The average active person has an MED (minimal erythemal dose) of twenty minutes, meaning that during the hours of strong sun they can stay out for about twenty minutes with no protection before beginning to show pink. Of course, people vary, some having MEDs as low as 5 minutes in certain kinds of torrid sun conditions, but twenty minutes was considered sufficient for most people, certainly for surfers who were used to the sun. An SPF (sun protection factor) of 3 means that a given individual's MED is multiplied by three if the sunscreen stays on the skin. A twenty-minute MED becomes one hour of protection with an SPF of 3 as long as the sunscreen does not wash off.

We targeted six hours of protection for our brand because that amount of time covers the dangerous hours of any day just about anywhere in the world any time of the year. That meant on average we needed an SPF of 18 to go with the water durability. At that time, an SPF of 15 was all that was allowed to be claimed by law (An FDA monograph governs this category. It states what testing has to be done, and what can be claimed in exact wording depending on test results. We successfully challenged this monograph even as a company with only three employees.)

We started by writing what I call Invention Guidelines, kind of a mini-backbone that guides product development. Essentially, those guidelines stated that if we had a formula that would protect an average surfer for six hours in and out of the water, we would be able to sell a lot of it. We wanted the formula to be concentrated so it could be sold in bottles small enough to go in gear bags, wet suits, and surfer trunks.

Those guidelines went on to speculate on such details as what the formula should be like, and even included the idea of a cosmetic flaw to reinforce performance. (A cosmetic flaw is the bad taste of Listerine.) The cosmetic flaw in Bullfrog was a slightly greasy feel to reinforce water durability. It turned out also to have a more important cosmetic flaw. It could sting the eyes if it got in them. A cosmetic flaw, by the way, is something that you introduce into a formula to make the expectation more believable. The best example is the taste of Listerine. If it tastes this bad it must work. The greasiness and stinging of Bullfrog helped users believe that it was strong and still on their skin.

No inventor who had ever worked in sunscreens thought it could be done, so we interviewed independent chemists who had never worked in the category. As I recall, we picked three, gave each the invention guidelines, enough funding to cover out-of-pocket costs, and a deadline for initial submissions. We promised that we would choose one of them based on the initial ideas and submissions, then work with him exclusively and that he would continue to have costs covered plus equity in the company.

We followed the same equity strategy for patent lawyers, package designers, etc. When we were ready to go, we had three pools of shares: founder shares, contributor shares, and investor shares. This is how we got so much development done for so little funding.

We tested the formulas with real surfers in real sea conditions. Greg Chelew, Don's son, put together the testing base, but we managed the test. Feedback came in, we made adjustments and retested. We continued this pattern until we had a formula we trusted. The resulting formula was distinctive and patentable. It was different in three ways from other sunscreens. One, it contained no water. Two, it was a solution, not an emulsion. Three, it had extremely small particle size for better skin coverage.

While this testing was going on, Don and I were constructing the Brand Backbone and Business Plan. Everything was determined up front from the research we were doing with surfers and with potential retailers.

The entire Brand Backbone Strategy was written before we started developing the name or any of the marketing elements like packaging, advertising copy, etc.

The money was raised from the Brand Backbone and Business Plan. We did not have the formula completed yet, and we did not know what we were going to name it yet. I still have the original Brand Backbone Strategy document, and it is for a "water durable sun block."

There were a number of elements in the Brand Backbone Strategy that are interesting within the context of the idea of Killer Brands.

First, our focus was singular: "water durability" to a degree never before possible. Second, we intended to build distribution and our user base without giving the retail trade a single penny in buying, promotion, or merchandising allowances. (This was in a category that did 85 percent of its volume on some kind of discount. I was lucky because my partner had never worked in consumer products before and didn't know that what we were attempting "could not be done.")

Third, we were going to ship or deliver all products directly to stores, no matter the channel, and use no trade warehouses. We were dependent upon retailer behavior with the brand and wanted to make sure that we were the only touch point with the retailers.

Fourth, we were going to tightly control distribution and not allow any off-strategy retailer to carry the brand, nor any retail store to have the brand in an area that was not yet receiving the brunt of the brand's marketing activities.

Fifth, we were going to expand distribution one beach area per week, sweeping up the California coast following the arrival of spring weather. We would sell and deliver beginning inventory from our own vehicles, and merchandise each store as we did so.

Sixth, we were going to spend every dime that we could against developing users, targeting the California surfing population in the first year, then expanding inward with additional sun-oriented activity groups in subsequent years. The expansion strategy called for rolling the brand out "like singing a round, and selling the brand to another company before we finished the song."

We ended up naming the brand Bullfrog Amphibious Formula Sun Block. We secured trademarks on both Bullfrog and on Amphibious Formula. The naming strategy called for finding a word uncommon in the category, a word that might become part of a surfer's jargon, and a word that connoted water durability. Hal Silverman, our package designer, wanted to call the brand Amphibious Formula. I liked the concept in that it stepped out of the approved FDA wording and provided a foundation for creating and owning something "beyond waterproof," but I couldn't see creating any excitement around the name Amphibious Formula. So we settled on Bullfrog as the brand name and Amphibious Formula as a descriptor, for which we also secured a registered trademark—not an easy position to secure, but Jay Geller, who is a great trademark lawyer, did it.

> A good name is uncommon to the product category, but still connotes something positive.

We introduced with Bullfrog invasion teaser ads in beach newspapers during the weeks preceding the arrival of the Bullfrog Amphibious Assault Vehicle in each beach area. The Assault Vehicle was an old Volkswagen bus painted Bullfrog green that served as our selling and marketing van. We would hit a beach community on Monday morning and call on stores all week.

The paper that week contained an ad announcing "Bullfrog Invasion Predicted to Hit Local Beaches This Week." The ad copy went something like this: "The massive invasion of amphibious bullfrogs that began sweeping up Southern California beaches a few weeks ago has now reached Redondo Beach. These are no ordinary bullfrogs. These bullfrogs love the sun and the haze, the wind and the waves. The invasion is usually preceded by the appearance of the Bullfrog Amphibious Assault Vehicle, which is said to resemble a large green Volkswagen bus. Watch for it."

The Amphibious Assault Vehicle had signage on it. The back said, "300,000 bullfrogs will be born in this van this year." There were waterproof boards on each side of the bus where we wrote the names of the stores that stocked Bullfrog, each right after they made the decision before we left their store. These stores were labeled the local Bullfrog hangouts. The van would pull up to a store, our salesman in his shorts and bullfrog T-shirt would get out with a prepack containing forty-eight one-ounce bottles of Bullfrog. He would make the pitch to the store owner or manager, show the advertising, and explain that we would hit local beaches that weekend and give single use "Tadpole" samples to every surfer we could see, together with Bullfrog fifty-cent credit cards (plastic waterproof coupons shaped just like credit cards) and personally tell them about the product. "Bullfrog stays on six hours in and out of the water. Won't wet off or sweat off."

If the retailer decided to buy the prepack, we would set up the counter display for them, tape a large green "waterproof" plastic banner in his window that said, "Bullfrog Sold Here," and then add his name to the Bullfrog Amphibious Assault Vehicle as a local Bullfrog hangout. The retailer's choice was simple. He could join the major event occurring on his beaches that weekend, or he could wait and miss it. About 70 percent of all accounts called on during that fourteen-week rollup of California beaches in Year 1 took Bullfrog in their stores on the first call with no buying allowance or cash incentive. The others just missed out. No bribery, just legitimate marketing excitement.

To add to the brand communications and to the excitement, we also left a sixteen-page mini-brochure, one for every bottle of Bullfrog, that was entitled "The Bullfrog Owner's Guide." This brochure told the whole story of the brand, from the trials of Greg Chelew to his surfer friends who served in the testing base (some of whom had great names like "Buttons Humphrey") to the meaning of MED to the many reasons why too much sun is bad for you. "There's a reason they called it tanned hide—looks good on a suitcase, pitiful on a person." The tonality of this Owner's Guide helped create the brand character for Bullfrog.

Following our beach event, we ran a full-page ad in the following week's local beach paper listing all of the local Bullfrog hangouts. We supported all of this with less specific "Bullfrog Invasion Sweeps North" ads in *Surfer* magazine.

At the end of that first summer, market research showed that Bullfrog unaided awareness among surfers in these fourteen California beach areas was 82 percent, and that 68 percent claimed Bullfrog as their regular brand. And it wasn't just surfers. Using surfers as the torture test started working immediately. I remember driving to the first store that had ordered a second prepack. It was the independent Bayshore Pharmacy in Newport Beach just off of Balboa Island. I pulled up and saw the Bullfrog Sold Here banner in the window. It was a very large drug store. I went to the pharmacy counter and there was the second Bullfrog prepack already half sold.

I asked the pharmacist, "How many surfers a week do you get in this store?" He answered, "None." I then asked, "How much beach traffic?" He answered, "Very little." I followed with, "Who then is buying this Bullfrog?" I will never forget his answer: "Little old ladies with blue hair." I knew we were off to the races.

In that first year, we spent $49,000 on advertising and sampling. We sold over $250,000 of product at full price, $3.00 per ounce. The retailer sold it for $5.00 per ounce. We never looked back.

The core expectation for Bullfrog was "water durable." That expectation was compelling to the target audience, which was surfers in the first year then expanded to other activity groups to whom the expectation was also compelling. The expectation itself was differentiated in degree and even in kind at that point in history. And of course the elements of the brand—the name, the packaging, the advertising—all helped differentiate the expectation.

The brand was more perfectly aligned than anything I had worked on prior to Bullfrog and probably better aligned than anything I have worked on since, even down to water-durable coupons and water-durable banners in store windows.

And the linkage was built right into the brand and everything that was done with it. Once you understood that this sun block was called Bullfrog because it was amphibious, that it worked in and out of the water, that it did not wet off or sweat off, you have the brand story and you remembered it forever.

We sold Bullfrog to Chattem, Inc. in 1986, twenty years ago. I still run into the brand in some heartwarming places—heartwarming at least to me, the creator. A few years ago Bobby, a concierge at the Mansfield Hotel in New York, told me he had grown up in Southern California. I asked Bobby if he had surfed. He said sure. I asked if he had ever heard of Bullfrog, and he pulled his Bullfrog credit card out of his wallet. He was thirty years old and still had his Bullfrog credit card in his wallet. He explained that he and his friends thought the credit card was worth more to keep than it was to turn in for fifty cents.

In four years, we built Bullfrog into a 26.7 percent share of the Southern California sunscreen market, the clear market leader. We sold every bottle at full price. We took no returns. At our peak we had no more than six people working in the company including Don Chelew and myself. Bullfrog was a true Killer Brand. It is a clear example of how powerful the three principles—Focus, Alignment, and Linkage—can be when you get them right.

The principles were powerful for Bullfrog. They were powerful for me. They can be powerful for you.

CONCLUSION

What We Have Learned Together

I have titled this summary "What We Have Learned Together" because I think I learned more writing this book than perhaps you will in having read it (though I hope you have learned quite a lot). Teaching has always been a great way for me to learn. I would have learned even more if this book could have been interactive.

And I would like it to be interactive for as long as you remain interested. Please direct questions and discussions directly to me at *www.franklaneltd.com*.

Now let's review both how the marketplace works and how Killer Brands work.

Here's a quick summary highlighting the words you need to know:

* Every dollar you will ever make depends on **Choice;** really, on a Chain of Choice that favors your product or service.
* Each choice will be made based on **Expectation.** If you can deliver the right expectation, you can get chosen.
* **Focus** is the one singular, differentiating, and powerfully compelling quality, the motivating Expectation, that your Killer Brand is going to become known for.
* **Alignment** is connecting everything that you do in perfect harmony to deliver that Focus consistently, every time and for every user, with nothing that detracts from the Focus or the Expectation you've created.
* **Linkage** is finding a way to get that Focus, that Expectation credited in the minds of your prospects to the name of your Killer Brand and to no other brand.

Five simple words, really. But incredibly powerful ones, when understood and executed properly.

You too can own a Killer Brand. It will change your life.

BRAND INDEX